S0-BDO-516

| DATE DUE | | | |
|---|---|---|---|
| | | | |
| | | | |
| | | | |
| | | | |
| | | | |
| | | | |
| | | | |
| | | | |
| | | | |
| | | | |
| | | | |
| | | | |
| | | | |

Return your book when it

**594**
**ART**

Arthur, Alex.

Shell.

**13207**

HIGH DESERT MIDDLE SCHOOL
LIBRARY

323668 01988          06734C          68

EYEWITNESS BOOKS

# SHELL

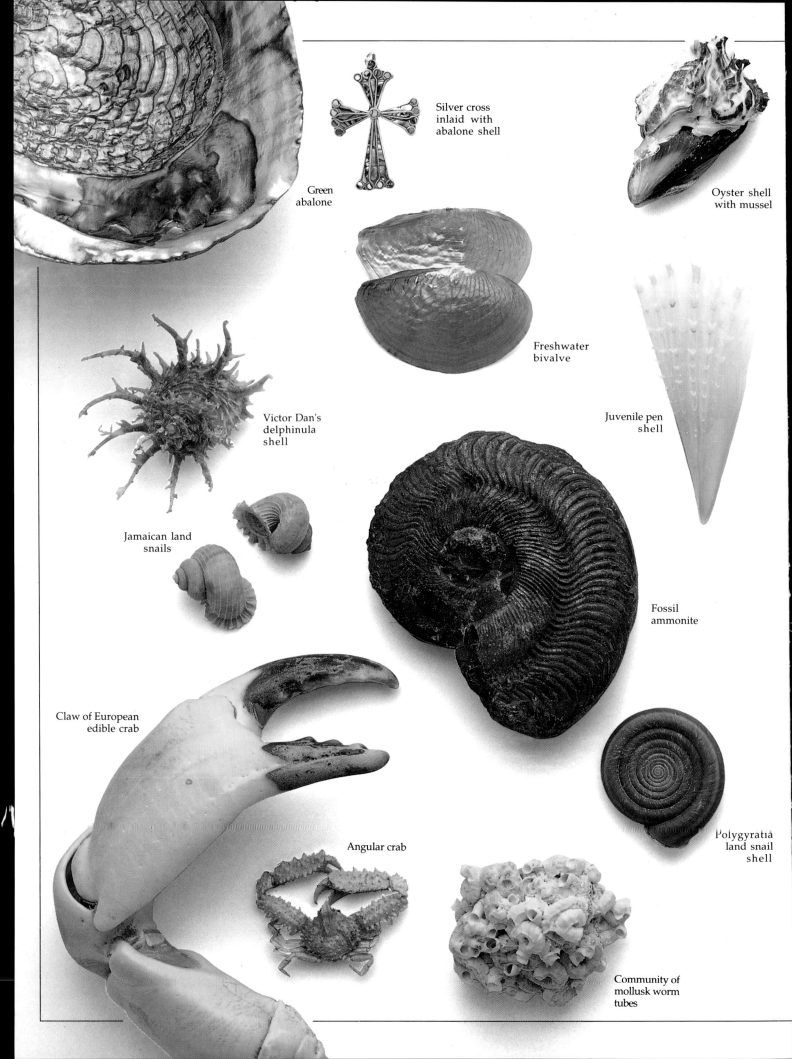

Green
abalone

Silver cross
inlaid with
abalone shell

Oyster shell
with mussel

Freshwater
bivalve

Juvenile pen
shell

Victor Dan's
delphinula
shell

Jamaican land
snails

Fossil
ammonite

Claw of European
edible crab

Polygyratia
land snail
shell

Angular crab

Community of
mollusk worm
tubes

Cuban land snails

Lamellose wentletraps

Precious wentletrap

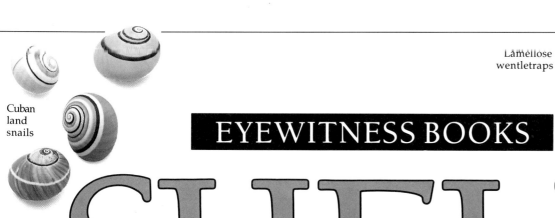

# EYEWITNESS BOOKS

# SHELL

Written by
Alex Arthur

HIGH DESERT MIDDLE SCHOOL
MEDIA CENTER

Venus comb murex

Japanese wonder shell

Cidaris sea urchin

Slate pencil sea urchin

Baby hawksbill turtle

ALFRED A. KNOPF • NEW YORK

Olla
volute
shell

Gibbula
shells

Cockle
shells

Scotch
bonnet

Deep-water
Pacific
phos

Harp
shell

Venus
shells

Hermit crab
in spiny
bonnet shell

Dublin Bay
prawn

This Eyewitness Book has been
conceived by Dorling Kindersley Limited
and Editions Gallimard

**Project editors** Tim Hammond, Susan McKeever
**Art editor** Julia Harris
**Natural history editor** Sophie Mitchell
**Managing editor** Vicky Davenport
**Managing art editor** Jane Owen
**Special photography** Andreas von Einsiedel, Dave King,
Colin Keates
**Editorial consultant** Dr. Gerald Legg

This is a Borzoi Book
published by Alfred A. Knopf, Inc.

Copyright © 1989 Dorling Kindersley Limited, London

All rights reserved under International and Pan-American
Copyright Conventions.
Published in the United States by Alfred A. Knopf,
Inc., New York. Distributed by Random House, Inc., New York.
Published in Great Britain by Dorling Kindersley Limited, London.
Manufactured in Singapore
0 9 8 7 6

Library of Congress Cataloging in Publication Data
Arthur, Alex
Shell/Written by Alex Arthur; photography by Andreas von
Einsiedel. p. cm - (Eyewitness Books)
Includes index.
Summary: Photographs and text examine different types of shells,
including seashells, eggshells, and fossil shells, focusing on such
aspects as how shells camouflage themselves and how they may
be collected.
1. Shells - Juvenile literature. [1. Shells.] I. von Einsiedel,
Andreas, ill. II. Title.
QL405.2.A77 1989 594'0471 - dc19 88-13449
ISBN 0-394-82256-0
ISBN 0-394-92256-5 (lib. bdg.)

Color reproduction by Colourscan, Singapore
Typeset by Windsor Graphics, Ringwood, Hampshire
Printed in Singapore by Toppan Printing Co. (S) Pte Ltd.

Blunted
demoulia
shells

# Contents

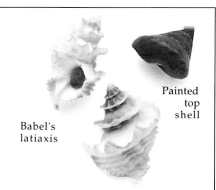

Babel's
latiaxis

Painted
top
shell

# What is a shell?

WHEN WE THINK OF A SHELL, we usually picture the pretty specimens that can be collected from the beach during a seaside stroll. In fact, "shell" can describe many different things. The word *shell* actually means a hard outer casing that encloses and protects a variety of things, from fruit to baby birds, from snails to scurrying crabs. A shell, sometimes no more than a hardened skin, sometimes a thick and heavy mollusk shell, is always a means of protection - against predators and mechanical damage, against extreme temperatures. Egg shells protect the unborn; nut shells enclose fruit and protect the seeds that give rise to new life. Many insects are protected by a hardened and segmented outer skin, and heavily thickened shells are found in crabs and lobsters. In living creatures like lobsters, the shell is called an exoskeleton, or external skeleton. One drawback of an exoskeleton is that it does not grow as the creature does, so the old shell must be shed and replaced by a new one big enough to accommodate its larger size.

**WORM SHELLS**
Even worms can make shells! This colony (left), found at the bottom of an estuary (inlet), contains hundreds of hard, coiling tubes. Each one was once the home of a tiny marine worm.

**HAIRY NUT**
The fruit of the tropical coconut palm (right) can be bought in most parts of the world to eat. A thick, hard, hairy shell, or husk, encases the sweet, milky juices and white flesh. A soft skin covers the coconut when growing; it is usually removed before selling.

*Hairs on husk*

*White acorn of nut*

*Shell*

*Seed*

**LUCKY BEANS**
Sea beans or "lucky" beans grow in pods, mainly along the banks of the Amazon River in South America. The pods burst and drop their beans into the river. The beans are carried to the sea and are polished by the salt water. They are often used as lucky charms.

Ostrich shell

**ARMORED ARMADILLO**
The armadillo is one of the last remaining types of a group of armor-plated animals that flourished on earth over 50 million years ago.

**EGG SHELLS**
Many creatures lay eggs in which their young can develop outside of the mother's body. The best known are those laid by birds. Fertilized eggs hatch into fledglings, like the baby pheasant above.

*Pheasant hatching*

**BIG BIRD**
At twenty times the size of a chicken egg, the ostrich egg is one of the largest eggs ever produced by a bird.

**SKULL OR SHELL?**
Unlike shells, skeletons are internal, and enclosed by skin and flesh. However, you can think of a skull as a type of shell, as it encloses and protects some soft organs, largely the brain, while at the same time providing a framework to support flesh and skin tissue. Mammals, birds, and reptiles all have internal skeletons, each one giving a creature its special shape.

Badger skull

*Pincer*

*Segmented body*

**SCORPION CASE**
Like all insects, scorpions are invertebrates (lacking a backbone) with a hardened outer casing that protects them. Insects are the most abundant of all creatures, and have long been thought to be closely related to the crustaceans (p. 22). Like crabs and lobsters, segmented and armored insects must shed their hardened casing in order to grow.

*Sting*

*Four pairs of walking legs*

# Creatures with shells

Of all the many different types of animals, only a few have a hard outer casing, or shell, to protect the internal organs of their bodies. Mammals, birds, reptiles, and fishes have developed an internal skeleton for this purpose. Tortoises, turtles, and terrapins are the only vertebrate (backboned) animals that have both an internal skeleton and an external shell. Most of the other shelled creatures are invertebrates, which means they have no backbones, and many are very simple animals that have remained virtually unchanged for millions of years. Not all shells are the same: seashells and snail shells are made from layers of calcium carbonate, crab shells are formed from a substance called chitin, while tortoise-shell is made from plates of bone covered by keratin - a protein found in human fingernails.

The nautilus

**LIVING DANGEROUSLY**
A tentacled head extends from the shell of the living nautilus. Unlike many other mollusks, the creature is not fully enclosed by its shell, and therefore cannot hide when danger threatens.

Nautilus shell

## Mollusks

The largest group of shelled creatures are the mollusks, of which there are over 75,000 species, including snails, oysters, and octopuses. These versatile animals have evolved to live in the sea, in fresh water, and on land. Most mollusks have some kind of protective shell.

Edible land snails

**SHELLED CEPHALOPOD**
This shell belongs to the nautilus - a member of the most advanced group of mollusks: the cephalopods (p. 19). The nautilus is the only kind of cephalopod that still has a true external shell.

**EDIBLE SNAIL**
One of the best-known shells is that of the edible land snail. These creatures are now quite rare in the wild but are commercially farmed and sold as a gourmet food.

Portuguese oyster

**INTERNAL SHELLS**
Some mollusks have developed shells that are not visible from the outside. These spirula shells belong to a squidlike mollusk.

Spirula shells

**SPINY SNAIL SHELL**
Like the edible snail, this murex (spiny shell) belongs to a group of single-shelled mollusks known as gastropods (p.12). This type of snail lives in the sea, where the variety of mollusks is greatest.

**JEWEL IN THE SHELL**
Pearls are formed inside oysters (p.36). These mollusks are known as bivalves - they have shells in two halves that are joined by an elastic ligament and held together by strong muscles. Edible oysters are farmed commercially like edible land snails (above).

Venus comb murex

# Reptiles

The reptiles are a varied group of cold-blooded vertebrate animals that includes snakes and lizards.
Only turtles, tortoises, and terrapins (p. 28) have shells, and these are really only extensions of their own skeletons.

**TORTOISE SHELL**
The bony shell of the tortoise makes a protective armor into which the animal can pull its head and legs in times of danger.

Moorish tortoise and shell

# Crustaceans

There are over 30,000 types of crustaceans, including lobsters, shrimps, crabs, and barnacles. Most crustaceans have some sort of jointed shell, or carapace, and live in the oceans, although some have adapted to life in fresh water and on land.

**EDIBLE CRAB**
In many parts of the world crab meat is considered a delicacy, and crabs are fished in large numbers using baited traps. The main shell of the crab protects the internal organs; the limbs are also covered in a hard, shell-like substance. This specimen has lost two of its eight legs.

**SEA URCHIN TEST**
The shell of a sea urchin is known as a test, and is made up of closely fitting plates that enclose the creature's soft parts.

Tropical sea urchin

Purple sea urchin

**A SPINY SKIN**
The tests of living sea urchins are covered with hundreds of spines that help the creature to move around on the sea bed. Sometimes these spines are very sharp.

# Echinoderms

This group of primitive sea-dwelling creatures includes starfish and sea cucumbers, which do not have shells, as well as sea urchins and sea potatoes (p. 20).

Florida sand dollar

**SAND DOLLARS**
These flattened sea urchins have very tiny spines and are adapted for life on sandy shores (p. 21).

Brown crab

**BROWN HAIRY CRAB**
This small crab lives in shallow-water rock pools, but relatives with leg spans of over 12 ft (3.5 m) can be found in deeper waters.

Atlantic barnacles

**BARNACLES**
Although they don't look much like crabs or lobsters, barnacles are also crustaceans. All barnacles are marine creatures and spend their lives attached to a hard base such as another shell or the hull of a boat. Barnacle shells are strengthened by plates made from calcium.

9

# Living in a whorl

DESPITE THE GREAT VARIETY in pattern, size, and weight, all seashells are made by the animals that live inside them, and all grow steadily outward. The whorl-shaped structures formed by the gastropod mollusks represent some of the most remarkable designs to be found anywhere in the natural world. Starting life as a tiny larva, the mollusk sets about building its shell by depositing calcium from the mantle - a fleshy fold on the animal's body. As the creature grows, the shell is extended outward in the form of a perfect spiral. Each type of seashell has a slightly different design, and this unique shape is passed on to each new generation.

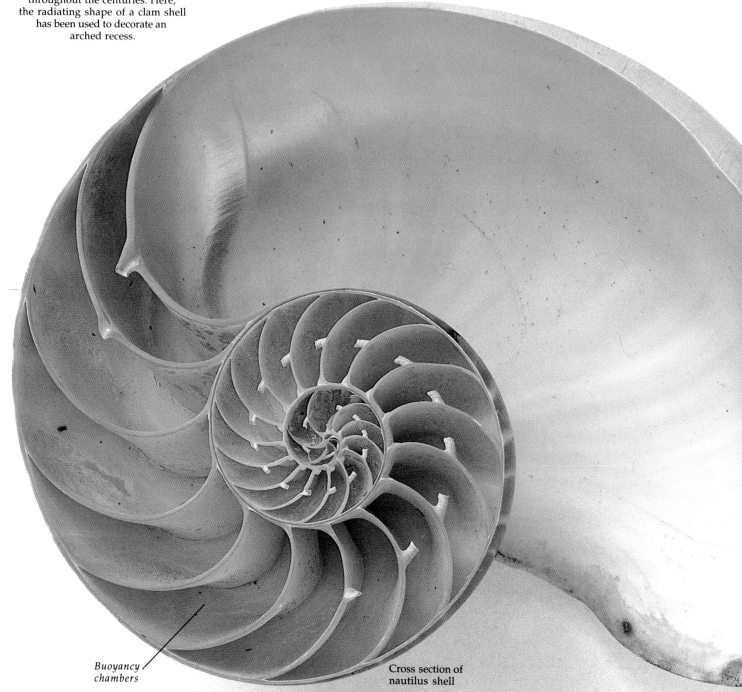

**SHELL INSPIRED ART**
The beautiful forms of seashells have influenced and inspired countless artists and architects throughout the centuries. Here, the radiating shape of a clam shell has been used to decorate an arched recess.

*Buoyancy chambers*

Cross section of nautilus shell

**Sundial shell
from below**

**Sundial shell
from above**

**SUNDIALS**
One of the most
perfectly symmetrical (even)
of all seashells is the sundial, or
architect shell. Its whorls grow
in a continuous, even curve.

Trapezium
horse conch

**SHELLY STAIRCASE**
Snail-like shells are built
in the same way as a
spiral staircase, with
the shell winding
downward around
a central shaft.

*Earliest
whorls*

*Whorls*

Cross section
of triton shell

*Central shaft,
or columella*

*Toothed
aperture
(opening)*

Cross section
of turban shell

*Siphonal
canal*

**INSIDE STORY**
Cutting a seashell in half allows us to
appreciate how it revolves around a
central pillar (pole). The nautilus shell
(opposite) is made differently from most
shells: each section of the spiral is
sealed off as the animal moves out
farther from the center.

# Snails of the world

Doris
harp shell

Delphinula
shell

**JAPANESE SHELLS**
These oddly shaped delphinula
shells come from
Japan.

IF YOU PICK UP A SEASHELL from the beach,
chances are you will have found the empty shell of
a sea snail. Snails belong to a large group of mollusks
otherwise known as gastropods, or univalve shells. Both
these names describe certain distinctive features: the
word *gastropod* is derived from the Greek words
for "stomach" and "foot" and, in simple terms, it is
around the massive foot of a snail that all its important organs are based. The term *univalve*
describes the single shell, often coiled in a spiral
shape, that many gastropods inhabit - as opposed
to the two-piece shells which are a feature of the bivalves (p. 16). The gastropods are the largest
group of mollusks, and there are more than 40,000
different types living in the world's seas.

**FRAGILE
FIGS**
The graceful and
extremely fragile fig
shell lives in warm
seas. When alive,
it covers much
of the shell
with its
body.

Bengal
fig shell

**TROPICAL
HARP SHELLS**
The beautiful harp
shell gets its name
from the smooth ribs
spaced regularly around
the shell, which resemble
the strings of a harp.

**THE COLOR PURPLE**
Purple dye can be made from
some mollusks, including certain
types of murex (spiny shells). The
ancient Phoenicians were the
first to discover this art, and
their Tyrian purple cloth -
named after the city of Tyre
where it was made - was
worn by Roman nobles
as a symbol of
their wealth. Purple
has been regarded as a
royal color ever since,
and the ceremonial robes
of many kings and queens are
still made of purple cloth to
this day.

**WARM-WATER FROGS**
So-called because of their roughly
textured appearance, frog shells
can be found in most warm
seas. Large specimens were
once used to make oil
lamps.

Geography
cone

**DEADLY POISON CONES**
Cone shells live in most seas and feed
mainly on small fish and worms. They
are among the most sought after of all
shells, and are well known for their
ability to paralyze their prey with
a tiny, barbed and poisonous "harpoon."
One of the most highly poisonous cone
shells is the geography cone from the
Indo-Pacific (Asian Pacific to Indian
Ocean). It has been responsible
for a number of human deaths.
Any cone shell you find should
be handled very carefully.

Noble
frog shell

Common
distorsio

**DISTORTED
DISTORSIOS**
Found mainly
in tropical seas,
the distorsio shell
has a strangely
inflated and distorted
appearance. These shells are
members of the triton family
(right) and are also closely
related to frog shells (above left).

**REAL CONCHES**
Many types of seashell are commonly
referred to as conch shells, but the name
really only applies to a family of
about 100 widely
distributed shells.
The best known
is the large
pink conch
from the
West Indies,
a shell that
is often
used as
food and
as an or-
nament.
Semi-
precious
pink pearls
have been
found inside
some shells.

Roman nobleman with
Tyrian purple cape

Trunculus
murex

Rose-branch
murex

Purple-dye
murex shells

Bubonian
conch

**SPINY
BEAUTIES**
There are many different
types of murex shells.
They are usually
decorated with
attractive frills
and spines.

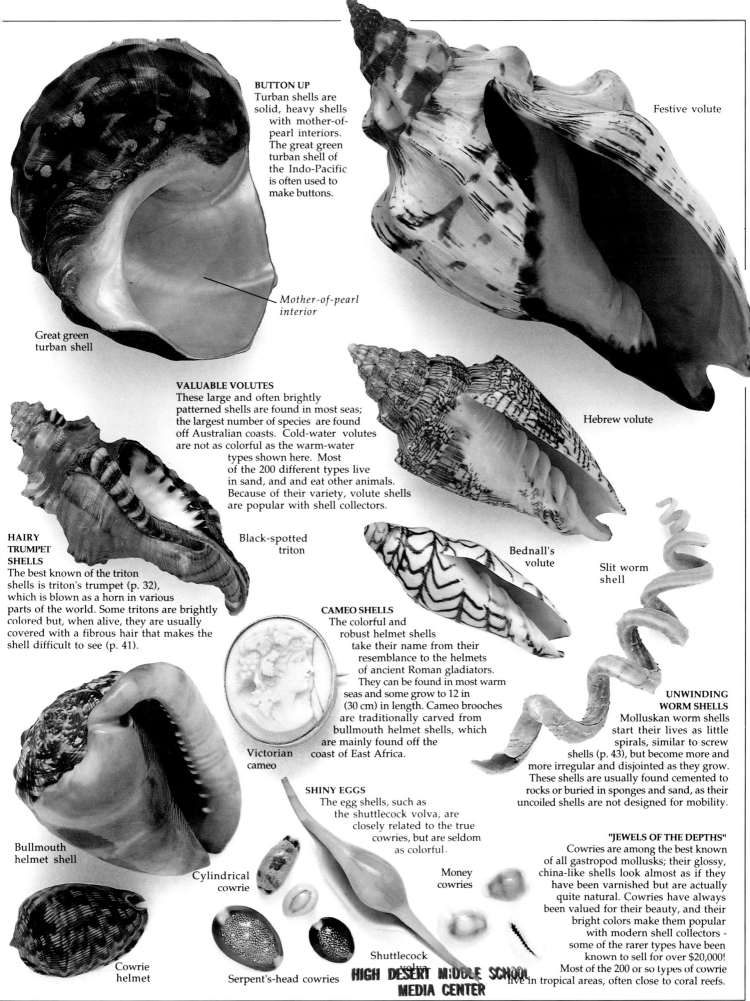

**BUTTON UP**
Turban shells are solid, heavy shells with mother-of-pearl interiors. The great green turban shell of the Indo-Pacific is often used to make buttons.

Festive volute

*Mother-of-pearl interior*

Great green turban shell

**VALUABLE VOLUTES**
These large and often brightly patterned shells are found in most seas; the largest number of species are found off Australian coasts. Cold-water volutes are not as colorful as the warm-water types shown here. Most of the 200 different types live in sand, and and eat other animals. Because of their variety, volute shells are popular with shell collectors.

Hebrew volute

**HAIRY TRUMPET SHELLS**
The best known of the triton shells is triton's trumpet (p. 32), which is blown as a horn in various parts of the world. Some tritons are brightly colored but, when alive, they are usually covered with a fibrous hair that makes the shell difficult to see (p. 41).

Black-spotted triton

Bednall's volute

Slit worm shell

**CAMEO SHELLS**
The colorful and robust helmet shells take their name from their resemblance to the helmets of ancient Roman gladiators. They can be found in most warm seas and some grow to 12 in (30 cm) in length. Cameo brooches are traditionally carved from bullmouth helmet shells, which are mainly found off the coast of East Africa.

Victorian cameo

**UNWINDING WORM SHELLS**
Molluskan worm shells start their lives as little spirals, similar to screw shells (p. 43), but become more and more irregular and disjointed as they grow. These shells are usually found cemented to rocks or buried in sponges and sand, as their uncoiled shells are not designed for mobility.

**SHINY EGGS**
The egg shells, such as the shuttlecock volva, are closely related to the true cowries, but are seldom as colorful.

**"JEWELS OF THE DEPTHS"**
Cowries are among the best known of all gastropod mollusks; their glossy, china-like shells look almost as if they have been varnished but are actually quite natural. Cowries have always been valued for their beauty, and their bright colors make them popular with modern shell collectors - some of the rarer types have been known to sell for over $20,000! Most of the 200 or so types of cowrie live in tropical areas, often close to coral reefs.

Bullmouth helmet shell

Cylindrical cowrie

Money cowries

Cowrie helmet

Serpent's-head cowries

Shuttlecock volva

HIGH DESERT MIDDLE SCHOOL MEDIA CENTER

*Continued on next page*

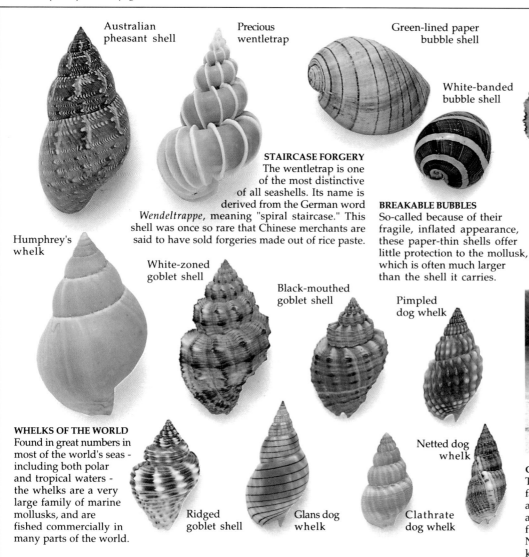

Australian pheasant shell

Precious wentletrap

Green-lined paper bubble shell

White-banded bubble shell

European china limpets

**STAIRCASE FORGERY**
The wentletrap is one of the most distinctive of all seashells. Its name is derived from the German word *Wendeltrappe*, meaning "spiral staircase." This shell was once so rare that Chinese merchants are said to have sold forgeries made out of rice paste.

**BREAKABLE BUBBLES**
So-called because of their fragile, inflated appearance, these paper-thin shells offer little protection to the mollusk, which is often much larger than the shell it carries.

**LUSTROUS LIMPETS**
Limpets are some of the best-known mollusks, being commonly found on coastal rocks, attached securely by their strong feet. Some types have a hole at the top of the shell and are known as keyhole limpets. The inside of a limpet shell often has an iridescent (rainbow-like) shine.

Humphrey's whelk

White-zoned goblet shell

Black-mouthed goblet shell

Pimpled dog whelk

Netted dog whelk

**WHELKS OF THE WORLD**
Found in great numbers in most of the world's seas - including both polar and tropical waters - the whelks are a very large family of marine mollusks, and are fished commercially in many parts of the world.

Ridged goblet shell

Glans dog whelk

Clathrate dog whelk

**GIANT PINK SEA SNAIL**
The mythical character Doctor Dolittle is famous for his ability to talk to animals of all kinds. In the film made about his adventures, the Doctor goes on a quest to find the fabulous giant pink sea snail. Needless to say, no mollusk has ever been known to reach this size!

# Freshwater snails

Most types of snail live in the sea, but many gastropods can also be found living in freshwater habitats. Some types absorb air from the water through gills; others have lungs and have to come to the surface to breathe. The patterns and colors of freshwater shells tend to be less vivid compared to those of marine species. Freshwater snails can be found living on weeds and rushes or in mud and sand; empty shells are often cast up on riverbanks, especially after flooding.

**GIANT AFRICAN RIVER SNAIL**
One of the largest freshwater snails occurs in the rivers of southeast Africa. Although it reaches a length of more than 5 in (12 cm), the shell of the giant African river snail is amazingly lightweight and fragile. In the sea, a shell of this size would normally be crusted with all sorts of growths, but in fresh water, shells usually have only a coat of algae that is easily removed.

**OUT OF AFRICA**
The strange-looking tiphorbia snail is just one of the hundreds of unique snail shells found in Lake Tanganyika in Africa. This huge expanse of landlocked water has developed a range of mollusks that are more like marine than freshwater gastropods.

**GREAT POND SNAIL**
This fragile snail is extremely common in lakes and ponds all over Europe. When alive, the shell has a greenish color; actually it is semi-transparent, and the green is the color of the mollusk inside.

Ram's-horn shell

**RAM'S-HORN SHELL**
The flattened spiral shape of the ram's-horn snail is fairly common.

**VIVIPAROUS SNAIL**
The viviparous banded snail, which has one of the largest shells of European fresh water snails, gives birth to live young.

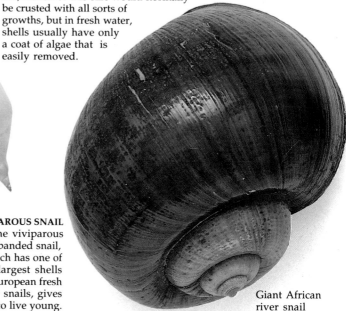

Giant African river snail

# Land snails

In order to survive, land snails need to remain moist, so they are usually most active at night or when it is cloudy or rainy. In dry conditions many types of snail can remain totally inactive for long periods, thereby retaining both energy and moisture. One museum specimen - thought to be long dead - was removed from a display case for cleaning, and began to move out of its shell after several years of "hibernation"!

**CHOOSY EATER**
Snails will eat most types of vegetation but are not especially keen on most healthy green garden plants.

**COLORFUL CUBAN COLLECTIBLES**
The brightly colored Cuban land snail is now protected by law because overcollecting has threatened the species' future.

*Cuban land snails*

**REGIONAL RARITY**
This extremely rare tropidophora snail is only found on the island of Madagascar in the Indian Ocean.

*Operculum*

**SNAILS IN TREES**
These typically bright-green snails are only found on Manus Island in the Pacific, and are on the official list of endangered species.

*Manus Island snails*

*Teeth*

**UPSIDE-DOWN SNAIL**
This unusual snail from the South American rain forest grows with its spiral facing earthward.

*Achatina snail*

**MASSIVE PEST**
The large achatina snails occur naturally in Africa, where they are eaten, but they are considered pests in other parts of the tropics where they have been introduced by humankind.

**LEFT-HANDED SNAIL**
Shells that coil in a counterclockwise direction are known as sinistral or left-handed shells - a feature that is relatively common among land snails.

*Left-handed Saõ Tomé snail*

*Growth scar*

*Operculum (lid over opening)*

**ELEPHANT SNAIL**
This strange-looking shell is found only in Malaya, and is so called because it is extremely heavy and robust.

*European striped snails*

*Common garden snails*

**BANDING TOGETHER**
The common European striped snail has a very variable pattern. The color and number of bands differ according to the kind of environment occupied by the snails (p. 41).

**COMMONER IN THE GARDEN**
Although abundant in gardens, snails do less harm than their cousins, the slugs.

# Homes with hinges

BIVALVES ARE AMONG THE BEST KNOWN of all marine creatures. Like the gastropods, bivalves are mollusks, but their shells are divided into two parts, or valves, that completely enclose and protect the soft body of the mollusk inside. The valves are connected by a shelly ridge or teeth that form a hinge, and can be opened and closed by strong muscles and ligaments. Compared to the gastropods, bivalves do not lead very active lives - unable to extend far out of their shells to crawl, many live embedded in sand and mud (p. 42), or remain hidden in rock crevices, while others attach themselves to a hard surface. Bivalves feed by opening their valves and filtering water through their gills to catch tiny creatures in the water around them. Bivalves can occur in vast numbers: some areas of the sea floor are known to contain as many as 8,000 living shells of one type in an area of 1.2 square yards (1 square meter).

**THE BIRTH OF VENUS**
This detail from the famous painting by Botticelli shows Venus being born from a scallop shell.

**Royal cloak scallop**

**SCURRYING SCALLOPS**
Scallops are among the best known bivalve mollusks. Some scallops have the ability to open and close their valves to swim away rapidly when disturbed.

Pacific thorny oyster

**SPINY OYSTER SHELL**
Spiny, or thorny, oysters are also known as chrysanthemum shells because of their likeness to the spiky-petaled flowers. Although not related to the true oyster, they are similar in that they remain attached to a solid base throughout their lives.

*Ligament*

**BUTTERFLY WINGS**
Shiny, colorful tellin shells are often washed ashore still in pairs, often resembling butterfly wings.

Flat tellin

Toothed donax

Thin tellin

**BEAN CLAMS**
Generally tiny and wedge-shaped, these creatures live in large numbers on warm-water beaches. Being so abundant, they are often used as food, especially in soups.

Noble pen shell

### SHELLY BATHTUB

The huge tridacna shell houses an animal that can feed up to twenty people! Common in the Molucca Islands, here it is being used as a child's bathtub.

### THE GIANT PEN SHELL

The pinna, or pen shell, spends its life in an upright position with its tapered end semi-embedded in soft bases, usually among weeds. The giant pen shell, which lives in the Mediterranean, is one of the largest bivalve mollusks, occasionally reaching a length of 2 ft (60 cm).

### OPEN AND SHUT CASE

Bivalves spend much of their lives with their valves slightly apart, and they must be able to close the gap quickly and securely to protect themselves from predators. For this purpose, the two halves of a bivalve shell match perfectly and, when shut, the opening can be just as hard to penetrate as the rest of the shell.

Cockscomb oyster

Spiny sand cockle

Fluted giant clam

Baby noble pen shell

### MINIATURE MAN-EATER

There are many different types and sizes of clams, but the biggest of all shelled mollusks is the giant clam, whose valves can measure 3.9 ft (1.2 m) and weigh over 1/4 ton (225 kg). These huge shells have been put to many uses by people, including bathtubs and feeding troughs, and the shell is so strong that it can be made into ax heads with which to fell trees. Living clams are said to have killed pearl divers by trapping their arms or legs between the two valves.

Byssal threads are secreted by some bivalves to anchor themselves to a hard base.

Byssus

# Strange seashells

Most seashells are either gastropods (p. 10) or bivalves (p. 16), but there are a few other groups of shelled creatures that look very little like either group. The smallest and least-known mollusk group is the gastroverms - rare creatures with small, limpet- shaped shells that can live 3 miles (5,000 m) below the surface of the sea. Better known are the chitons, sometimes referred to as coat-of-mail shells because the shells are made up of eight separate plates. Scaphopods, or tusk shells as they are commonly called, have shells that look like elephants' tusks. Like the chitons, these mollusks are primitive creatures that can be found in most of the world's seas, even in shallow water. The most advanced of all the mollusks are the cephalopods (from the Greek words for "head" and "foot") - so-called because of their distinctive tentacled heads. This class includes the octopus, squid, cuttlefish, and nautilus - mostly free-swimming creatures that have evolved without true shells.

**PARTS OF A CHITON**
The shell of a chiton consists of eight plates, or valves, which are attached to the back of the soft-bodied animal. These valves are joined and surrounded by a stretchy muscular band known as a girdle, allowing the animal to move over irregular surfaces. When a chiton is detached from its ground, it curls up to protect its soft body.

*Individual valves of a chiton*

Olive chitons

*Girdle*

**HOLDING ON TIGHT**
Chitons are found living on solid objects such as rocks and other shells. Like limpets, they hold on tight to the surface when disturbed.

*Shelly plates*

Underside of a chiton shell

**SIZEABLE VARIETY**
There are over 600 types of chiton and, although they are all roughly the same shape, they can vary greatly in size, from 0.1 in (.25 cm) to over 12 in (30 cm) long.

**TUSK SHELLS**
Tusk shells live with their heads buried in sand or mud. They feed on micro-scopic organisms that they catch and pass to their mouth with club-shaped tentacles.

*Shell*

*Feeding tentacles*

*Foot*

*Mantle*

Common tusk shells

Elephant's tusk shell

**VALUABLE ASSETS**
The ivory tusks of elephants have always been highly prized, but tusk shells, too, were once valuable. Like the famed money cowries (p. 13), once used as currency in Africa and the South Pacific, strings of tusk shells were used as money and jewelry by some North American Indian tribes.

*Sensory and feeding tentacles*

Green tusk shells

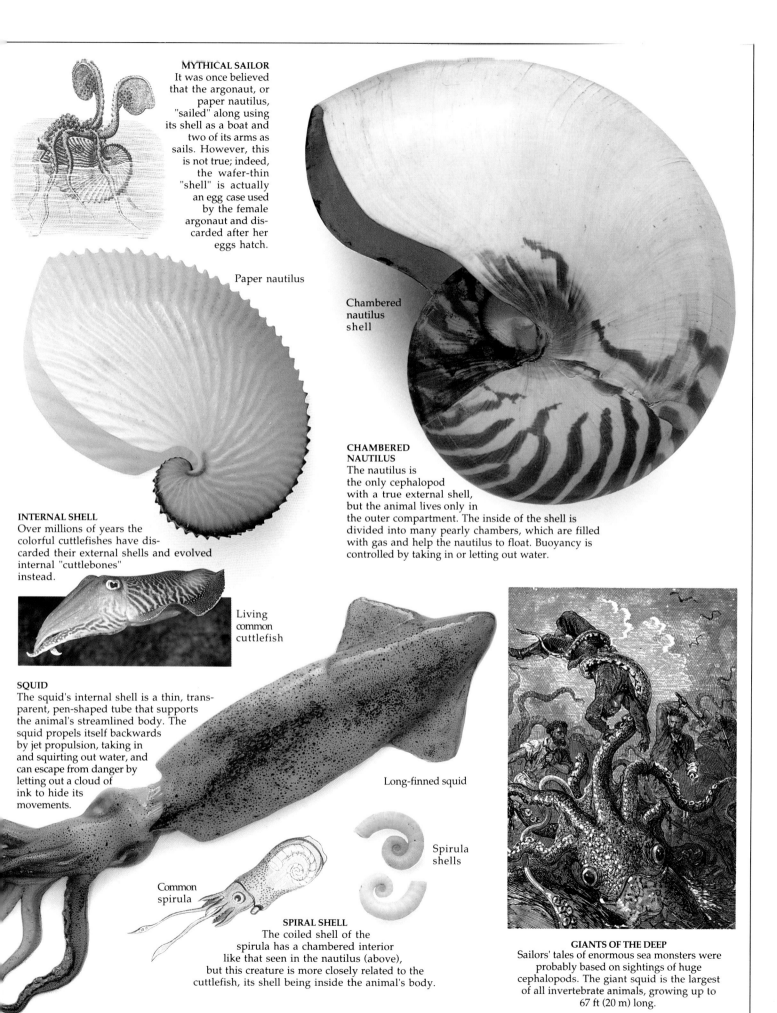

**MYTHICAL SAILOR**
It was once believed that the argonaut, or paper nautilus, "sailed" along using its shell as a boat and two of its arms as sails. However, this is not true; indeed, the wafer-thin "shell" is actually an egg case used by the female argonaut and discarded after her eggs hatch.

Paper nautilus

Chambered nautilus shell

**CHAMBERED NAUTILUS**
The nautilus is the only cephalopod with a true external shell, but the animal lives only in the outer compartment. The inside of the shell is divided into many pearly chambers, which are filled with gas and help the nautilus to float. Buoyancy is controlled by taking in or letting out water.

**INTERNAL SHELL**
Over millions of years the colorful cuttlefishes have discarded their external shells and evolved internal "cuttlebones" instead.

Living common cuttlefish

**SQUID**
The squid's internal shell is a thin, transparent, pen-shaped tube that supports the animal's streamlined body. The squid propels itself backwards by jet propulsion, taking in and squirting out water, and can escape from danger by letting out a cloud of ink to hide its movements.

Long-finned squid

Spirula shells

Common spirula

**SPIRAL SHELL**
The coiled shell of the spirula has a chambered interior like that seen in the nautilus (above), but this creature is more closely related to the cuttlefish, its shell being inside the animal's body.

**GIANTS OF THE DEEP**
Sailors' tales of enormous sea monsters were probably based on sightings of huge cephalopods. The giant squid is the largest of all invertebrate animals, growing up to 67 ft (20 m) long.

**19**

# Urchins of the sea

From below, the distinctive jaws of this living sea urchin are clearly visible.

THE SEA URCHINS belong to a large group of creatures called echinoderms, a word derived from the Greek words for "spiny" and "skin." Various types of odd-looking creatures with strange-sounding names belong to this group, which includes the starfishes and the sea cucumbers, but the sea urchins, sea potatoes, sea biscuits, and sand dollars are the only ones with shells. There are some 800 types of sea urchin living on the bottom of the world's oceans today. Although ancient in origin, they have adapted to most kinds of marine environment, from the polar regions to the tropics. They can be found in shallow or very deep water, and feed on both plants and animals. Echinoderms often show a five-rayed symmetry (evenness) in their bodies, a feature that is particularly clear in starfish-type animals.

Tropical sea urchin tests

**SEA URCHIN TESTS**
The shell of a sea urchin is known as a test and is made up of a series of plates that join each other or sometimes overlap. The test encloses and protects the soft parts of the animal. It is often shaped like a slightly flattened ball, and usually divided into five main areas. Sea urchin tests are often very colorful, and range in size from under 0.5 in (1 cm) to over 6 in (15 cm) in diameter.

Pea urchins

The smallest urchins of Europe's seas, these pea urchins are commonly found in beach debris.

**SPIKY OR SPINELESS?**
When alive, sea urchins are covered with numerous spines and tube feet that help the animal to move around. The spines are secured to the test by muscles around raised areas on the shell, which form a "ball-and-socket" joint that allows them to move in all directions. The spines on a sea urchin are used for locomotion, protection, and sometimes even as digging tools to burrow into rocks.

Sea urchin with all its spines

This edible sea urchin is the largest of Europe's urchins.

Sea urchin test exposed when spines removed

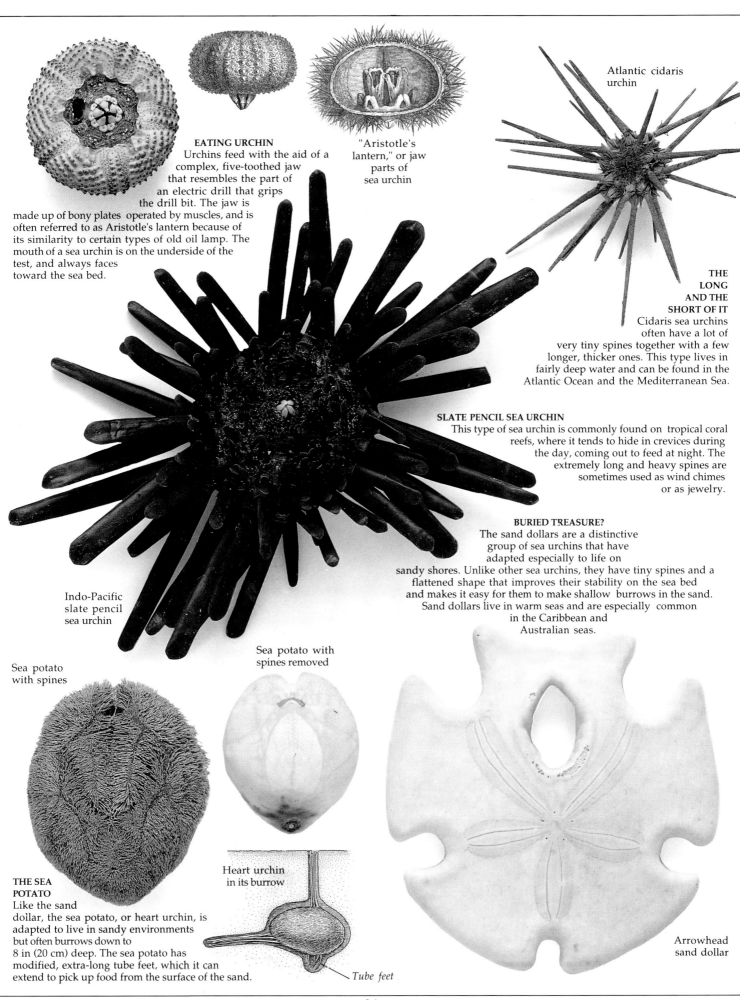

## EATING URCHIN
Urchins feed with the aid of a complex, five-toothed jaw that resembles the part of an electric drill that grips the drill bit. The jaw is made up of bony plates operated by muscles, and is often referred to as Aristotle's lantern because of its similarity to certain types of old oil lamp. The mouth of a sea urchin is on the underside of the test, and always faces toward the sea bed.

"Aristotle's lantern," or jaw parts of sea urchin

Atlantic cidaris urchin

## THE LONG AND THE SHORT OF IT
Cidaris sea urchins often have a lot of very tiny spines together with a few longer, thicker ones. This type lives in fairly deep water and can be found in the Atlantic Ocean and the Mediterranean Sea.

## SLATE PENCIL SEA URCHIN
This type of sea urchin is commonly found on tropical coral reefs, where it tends to hide in crevices during the day, coming out to feed at night. The extremely long and heavy spines are sometimes used as wind chimes or as jewelry.

## BURIED TREASURE?
The sand dollars are a distinctive group of sea urchins that have adapted especially to life on sandy shores. Unlike other sea urchins, they have tiny spines and a flattened shape that improves their stability on the sea bed and makes it easy for them to make shallow burrows in the sand. Sand dollars live in warm seas and are especially common in the Caribbean and Australian seas.

Indo-Pacific slate pencil sea urchin

Sea potato with spines removed

Sea potato with spines

Heart urchin in its burrow

Tube feet

## THE SEA POTATO
Like the sand dollar, the sea potato, or heart urchin, is adapted to live in sandy environments but often burrows down to 8 in (20 cm) deep. The sea potato has modified, extra-long tube feet, which it can extend to pick up food from the surface of the sand.

Arrowhead sand dollar

# Armor-plated animals

WHILE MANY CREATURES HAVE DEVELOPED strong outer casings that we call shells to protect their soft inner parts, one group has evolved what is more like a very hard and thick layer of skin. This large group is called the crustaceans, of which there are over 30,000 different types - including lobsters, crabs, and crayfish - mostly living in the sea. Most of the crustaceans possess shells that are jointed - a bit like the suits of armor worn by 15th-century knights. Until recently, the crustaceans were thought to belong to the group known as the arthropods - the largest group of living creatures - which includes all the various types of insects. Now the crustaceans are considered by many experts to have evolved separately many millions of years ago. There are, however, many similarities between the two groups - including segmented bodies, jointed limbs, and the hardened outer skeleton, or shell, that is shed from time to time to allow the animal to grow.

**THE LOBSTER IN ART**
Lobsters have pleased food lovers and inspired artists as well. This detail is from a 17th-century painting, *Still Life with Lobster*, by Joris Van Son.

*Tailpiece, or telson*

*Abdomen divided into six segments, or somites*

**STRONG WHEN INTACT**
Because of the way in which the segments of its body are joined together, a lobster can only swim backward or forward - it cannot twist sideways. The shelly somites are made from a protein known as chitin, which is strengthened by deposits of calcium salts. The somites are much softer at the joints, to allow the animal to move. In order to grow, the lobster must occasionally shed its shell and grow a new one. This makes it extremely vulnerable to enemies and the lobster wisely hides away until its new shell has had time to harden.

**COPYCAT CASING**
Like the lobster, the knights of old sacrificed flexibility in return for a protective suit of armor.

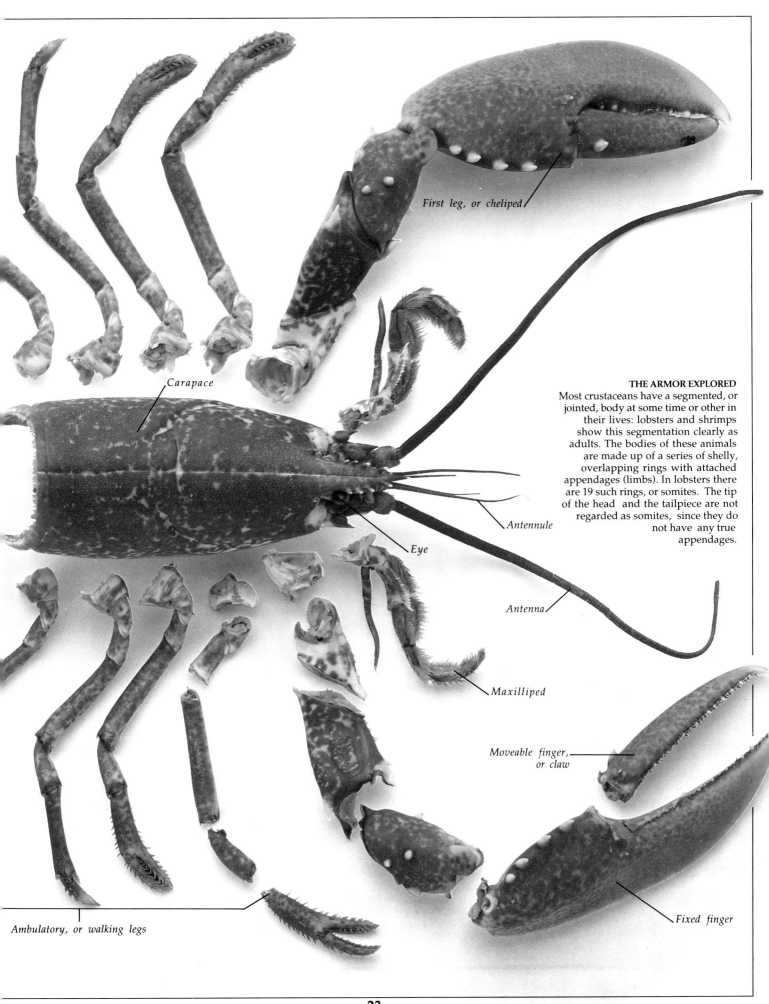

First leg, or cheliped

Carapace

Antennule

Eye

**THE ARMOR EXPLORED**
Most crustaceans have a segmented, or jointed, body at some time or other in their lives: lobsters and shrimps show this segmentation clearly as adults. The bodies of these animals are made up of a series of shelly, overlapping rings with attached appendages (limbs). In lobsters there are 19 such rings, or somites. The tip of the head and the tailpiece are not regarded as somites, since they do not have any true appendages.

Antenna

Maxilliped

Moveable finger, or claw

Fixed finger

Ambulatory, or walking legs

# Shells with ten legs

PERHAPS THE MOST familiar crustaceans are crabs, lobsters, shrimps, and crayfish. They all have the characteristic hardened, jointed shells, and ten legs, giving them the collective name of "decapods." But within the group crustacea, there is so much variety that it is impossible to find one feature common to every creature in the group that separates it from all other creatures. The members of the group range from tiny water fleas that live mainly in fresh water, to ostracods with their glow-in-the-dark bodies (p. 54 ); parasitic and limpet-like copepods, sometimes known as fish lice, that attach themselves firmly to their hosts; and even the heavily armored barnacles. Many of these creatures are microscopic and form a large part of plankton - the drifting life of the oceans. Plankton occurs in huge numbers in the world's oceans and is an important part of the marine food chain, eaten by creatures that range in size from tiny mollusks to huge whales.

**ALIVE AND SWIMMING**
Crab larvae, like the common crab larva above, are free-swimming. Newly hatched at under .039 in (1 mm) long, the larva looks more like a mosquito than a crab.

**MEAN FIDDLER**
Called the fiddler crab because the claws of the male look like a bow and fiddle, this creature lives in sandy burrows and sandy mud.

*Large claw is used to frighten enemies*

*Pincer claws used for catching and holding prey as well as for defense*

**NO WAY OUT**
Fishing for crabs and lobsters simply involves setting traps and waiting. The crab or lobster pots usually have two holes which get smaller toward the center of the basket. Crabs and lobsters, attracted by the bait within, crawl in and then are unable to get out, and have no choice but to await their fate.

19th-century engraving showing crab and lobster fishing scene on a beach

**A NEW SUIT**
Crabs, like all crustaceans, must shed their skins, or molt, in order to grow. At the time of molting, cracks appear in a crab's shell, and the creature's soft parts begin to come through, gradually pushing aside the old shell. Crabs in the process of molting are called peelers by fishermen and, when caught, are kept in tanks until they have molted, so that they can be sold as "soft-shells" - a delicacy for the gourmet. Soft-shells usually eat their old shells, as the land crab on the right is demonstrating.

*Pointed feet help crab to dig under sand*

Long walking legs

Unlike other crabs,
the spider crab
can walk diagonally
as well as sideways

**SPINY SPIDER**
With their long limbs and small
bodies, it is easy to see how spider
crabs got their name (p. 55). The
spiny spider crab (right) is one of
the largest European crabs and is
caught for food. Similar spider
crabs can be found around most of the
world - the coasts around Australia
boast almost 100 different species.
Despite their long legs, spider crabs
are slow-moving and make easy prey.

Spiny
carapace

Spiny spider crab

**COMBING THE OCEANS**
Unable to move about like their relatives the crabs
and lobsters, barnacles must rely on the surrounding
waters for nourishment. They feed by extending
their long, feathery legs from their shells and
"combing" the water for tiny food particles.

*Continued on next page*

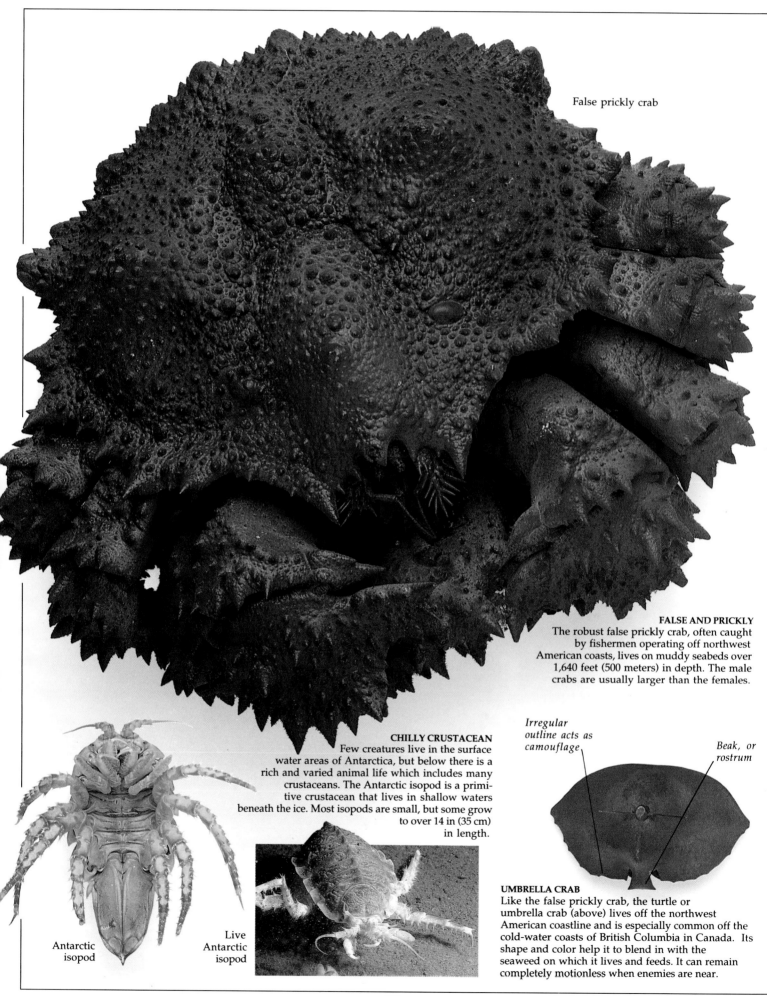

False prickly crab

**FALSE AND PRICKLY**
The robust false prickly crab, often caught by fishermen operating off northwest American coasts, lives on muddy seabeds over 1,640 feet (500 meters) in depth. The male crabs are usually larger than the females.

**CHILLY CRUSTACEAN**
Few creatures live in the surface water areas of Antarctica, but below there is a rich and varied animal life which includes many crustaceans. The Antarctic isopod is a primitive crustacean that lives in shallow waters beneath the ice. Most isopods are small, but some grow to over 14 in (35 cm) in length.

Irregular outline acts as camouflage

Beak, or rostrum

Antarctic isopod

Live Antarctic isopod

**UMBRELLA CRAB**
Like the false prickly crab, the turtle or umbrella crab (above) lives off the northwest American coastline and is especially common off the cold-water coasts of British Columbia in Canada. Its shape and color help it to blend in with the seaweed on which it lives and feeds. It can remain completely motionless when enemies are near.

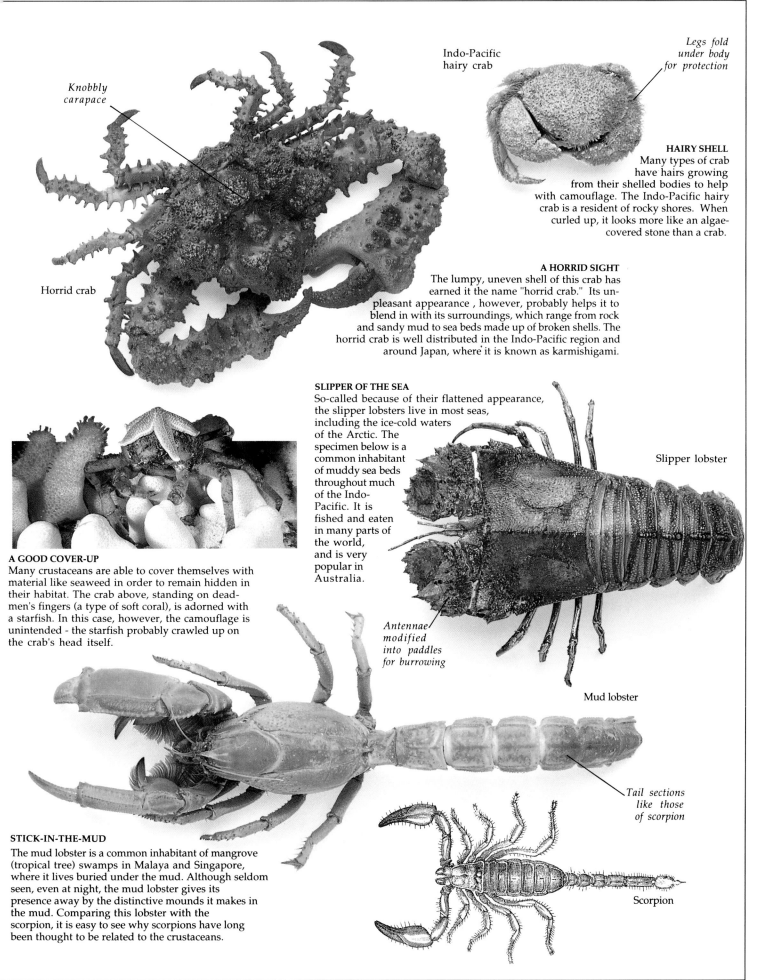

*Knobbly carapace*

Horrid crab

Indo-Pacific hairy crab

*Legs fold under body for protection*

**HAIRY SHELL**
Many types of crab have hairs growing from their shelled bodies to help with camouflage. The Indo-Pacific hairy crab is a resident of rocky shores. When curled up, it looks more like an algae-covered stone than a crab.

**A HORRID SIGHT**
The lumpy, uneven shell of this crab has earned it the name "horrid crab." Its unpleasant appearance , however, probably helps it to blend in with its surroundings, which range from rock and sandy mud to sea beds made up of broken shells. The horrid crab is well distributed in the Indo-Pacific region and around Japan, where it is known as karmishigami.

**SLIPPER OF THE SEA**
So-called because of their flattened appearance, the slipper lobsters live in most seas, including the ice-cold waters of the Arctic. The specimen below is a common inhabitant of muddy sea beds throughout much of the Indo-Pacific. It is fished and eaten in many parts of the world, and is very popular in Australia.

Slipper lobster

**A GOOD COVER-UP**
Many crustaceans are able to cover themselves with material like seaweed in order to remain hidden in their habitat. The crab above, standing on deadmen's fingers (a type of soft coral), is adorned with a starfish. In this case, however, the camouflage is unintended - the starfish probably crawled up on the crab's head itself.

*Antennae modified into paddles for burrowing*

Mud lobster

*Tail sections like those of scorpion*

**STICK-IN-THE-MUD**
The mud lobster is a common inhabitant of mangrove (tropical tree) swamps in Malaya and Singapore, where it lives buried under the mud. Although seldom seen, even at night, the mud lobster gives its presence away by the distinctive mounds it makes in the mud. Comparing this lobster with the scorpion, it is easy to see why scorpions have long been thought to be related to the crustaceans.

Scorpion

# Turtles, tortoises, and terrapins

Turtles, tortoises, and terrapins are an ancient and closely related family, having lived on this planet since the age of the dinosaurs. Being reptiles, they are vertebrates like us, but are unique in the animal kingdom in that they have a solid outer shell as well as an internal skeleton. They are also cold-blooded creatures, unable to regulate their body temperature internally. They can, however, raise their body temperature by basking in the sun. Most tortoises in the wild tend to live in the warmer parts of the world. Tortoises can be found in colder areas, too, but they then need to hibernate during the winter months. Although they seem very similar, tortoises, turtles, and terrapins have evolved to suit different environments: tortoises usually live on land, terrapins in freshwater, and all turtles but one live in the sea.

**THE HARE AND THE TORTOISE**
Tortoises are famous for their slow movements, but as the well-known fable "The Hare and the Tortoise" tells us, determination is more important than speed. Despite its slowness, the tortoise has managed to survive on earth with very little change for over 250 million years, relying mainly on its hard shell for protection.

Stinkpot turtle

Red-eared slider

Painted turtle

**BASKING TERRAPINS**
Terrapins live in freshwater habitats and can often be seen basking in the sun on rocks or riverbanks. Usually smaller than either tortoises or turtles, these endearing little creatures are often kept as pets in freshwater tanks.

*Clawed foot*

*Scutes, or scales, cover bony carapace*

On the Galapagos Islands in the Pacific live "giant" tortoises that can reach one-and-a-half metres (4.92 ft) in length.

*Plastron*

**TORTOISE TALE**
The armor-plated tortoise has a distinctive domed shell, or carapace, on top and a flat, bony plate, called a plastron, below. This plate protects most of the animal's soft tissues, and its exposed legs and head can be drawn quickly inside the shell when danger threatens. The tortoise does not have teeth but can still inflict a painful bite with the aid of its strong jaws and the sharp, horny tissue that surrounds them, like the beak of a bird.

## TORTOISE EXPOSED

From below, once the animal and the plastron or undershell have been removed, you can see clearly how the carapace of a chelonian (the group name for all turtles, tortoises, and terrapins) is really just an extension of its rib cage. Because its ribs are fused with its shell, the tortoise is unable to expand its lungs and must rely on the movements of its head and limbs to pump in fresh air. The tortoise is similar to its cousin the turtle, but the turtle has a less domed, more streamlined shell and webbed feet for fast swimming.

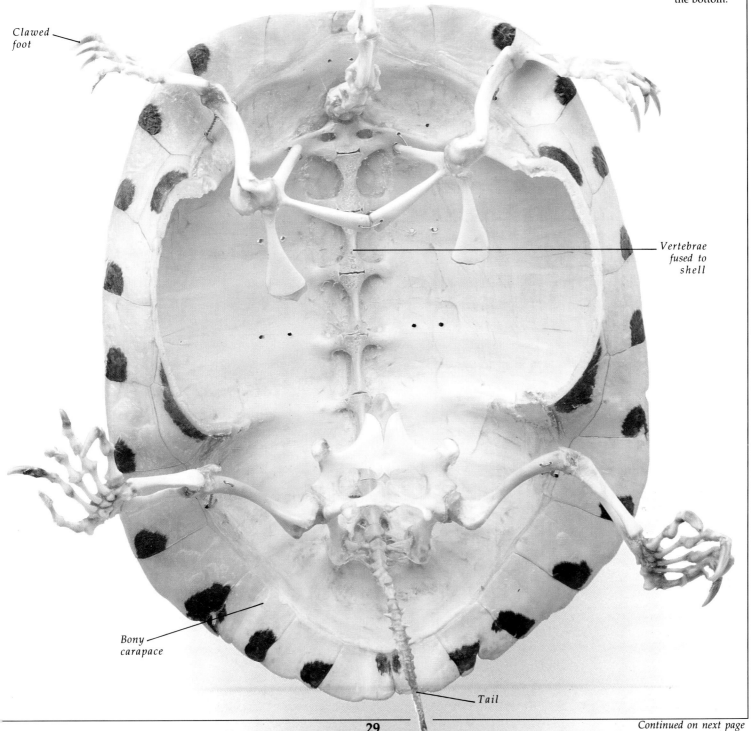

*Skull*

*Neck vertebra*

*Clawed foot*

*Vertebrae fused to shell*

*Bony carapace*

*Tail*

### A LEATHER SHELL?

The largest of all living turtles, this giant has a leathery, ridged skin above and below its body, instead of the usual horny plates, hence the name "leatherback." It tends to live in the middle of the sea, rather than the bottom.

*Continued on next page*

Continued from previous page

# Tortoiseshell designs

There are over 200 different types of tortoise, turtle, and terrapin, all belonging to a reptilian group called the Chelonia. Although the structure of the shell is essentially the same in most of the creatures in this group, the markings on the bony scales that make up the carapace are often very distinctive and provide a useful means of identification. As with most living creatures, the coloration of young specimens is different than that of adults.

**MOCK TURTLE**
In Lewis Carroll's story *Alice's Adventures in Wonderland*, Alice encounters many strange creatures on her travels, one of which is the melancholy Mock Turtle. Encouraged by the Gryphon, the Mock Turtle teaches Alice how to dance the famous Lobster Quadrille, and tearfully laments the fact that he is not a true turtle. This leads him to sing "Turtle Soup," a sad reminder that his days are numbered.

Young leopard tortoise carapace

Juvenile leopard tortoise carapace

**LEOPARD BY NAME, TORTOISE BY NATURE**
The leopard tortoise gets its name from the speckled markings on its domed shell. The young shells (above and left) have not yet developed the distinctive pattern visible on the adult (far left). Although widely distributed on the African continent, the leopard tortoise prefers savannah and woodland areas, where it feeds on a variety of plants.

**AN EXTRA WEIGHT**
As if the weight of its own enormous shell were not enough to carry, this giant tortoise is also bearing the load of Lord Rothschild, the world-famous 19th-century naturalist. Giant tortoises were first discovered by Charles Darwin on his voyage to the Galapagos Islands, and they have fascinated naturalists ever since. Lord Rothschild was especially fond of these slow-moving creatures, and kept many at his museum in Tring, England.

*Main carapace color is yellow*

Mature leopard tortoise carapace

During the late 19th and early 20th century, it was fashionable to own objects sculpted from tortoiseshell. The most beautiful tortoiseshell comes from the hawksbill turtle.

19th-century tortoiseshell hair comb

1920s tortoise-shell box

19th-century "lorgnette" glasses made from tortoiseshell

**GLIDING WITH EASE**
Hawksbill turtles are extremely fast swimmers, their long, paddle-like flippers and low shells helping them to glide smoothly through the water. Marine turtles come ashore to lay their eggs, and on land they are even slower than tortoises.

*Thick overlapping plates*

Natural hawksbill tortoiseshell

# Hawksbill turtles

One of the best known of all marine turtles is the hawksbill. Once hunted for its beautiful shell (above), this turtle is now on the official list of endangered species and imports are banned in many countries. It can be found in most warm seas around the world and feeds on mollusks and crustaceans.

# A growing shell

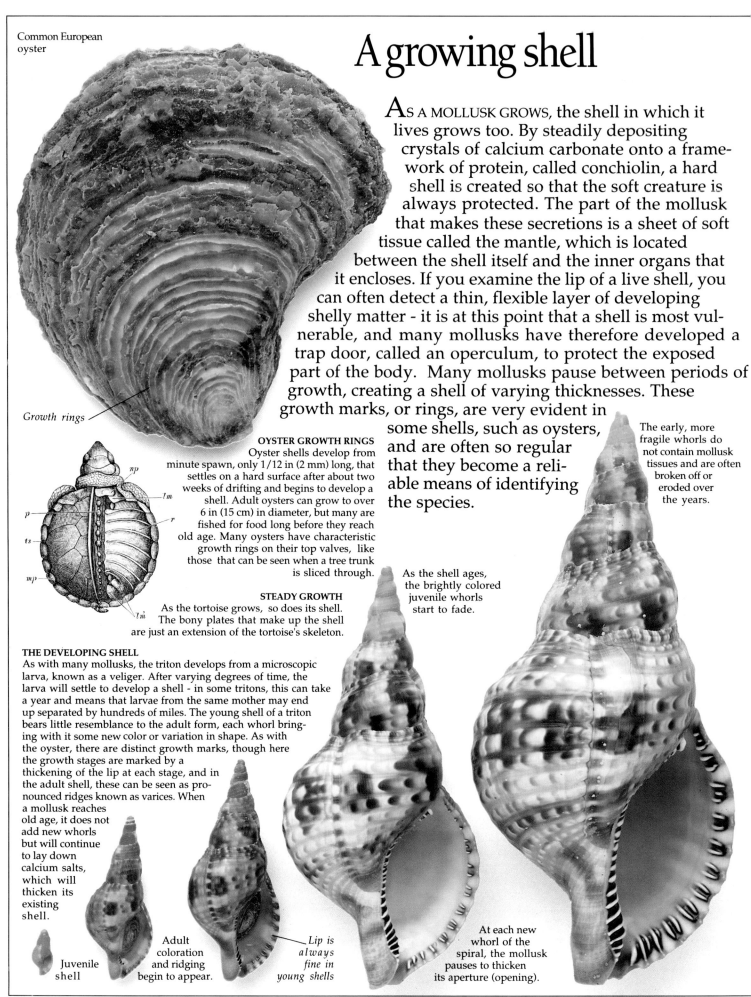

Common European oyster

*Growth rings*

As a MOLLUSK GROWS, the shell in which it lives grows too. By steadily depositing crystals of calcium carbonate onto a framework of protein, called conchiolin, a hard shell is created so that the soft creature is always protected. The part of the mollusk that makes these secretions is a sheet of soft tissue called the mantle, which is located between the shell itself and the inner organs that it encloses. If you examine the lip of a live shell, you can often detect a thin, flexible layer of developing shelly matter - it is at this point that a shell is most vulnerable, and many mollusks have therefore developed a trap door, called an operculum, to protect the exposed part of the body. Many mollusks pause between periods of growth, creating a shell of varying thicknesses. These growth marks, or rings, are very evident in some shells, such as oysters, and are often so regular that they become a reliable means of identifying the species.

**OYSTER GROWTH RINGS**
Oyster shells develop from minute spawn, only 1/12 in (2 mm) long, that settles on a hard surface after about two weeks of drifting and begins to develop a shell. Adult oysters can grow to over 6 in (15 cm) in diameter, but many are fished for food long before they reach old age. Many oysters have characteristic growth rings on their top valves, like those that can be seen when a tree trunk is sliced through.

**STEADY GROWTH**
As the tortoise grows, so does its shell. The bony plates that make up the shell are just an extension of the tortoise's skeleton.

**THE DEVELOPING SHELL**
As with many mollusks, the triton develops from a microscopic larva, known as a veliger. After varying degrees of time, the larva will settle to develop a shell - in some tritons, this can take a year and means that larvae from the same mother may end up separated by hundreds of miles. The young shell of a triton bears little resemblance to the adult form, each whorl bringing with it some new color or variation in shape. As with the oyster, there are distinct growth marks, though here the growth stages are marked by a thickening of the lip at each stage, and in the adult shell, these can be seen as pronounced ridges known as varices. When a mollusk reaches old age, it does not add new whorls but will continue to lay down calcium salts, which will thicken its existing shell.

The early, more fragile whorls do not contain mollusk tissues and are often broken off or eroded over the years.

As the shell ages, the brightly colored juvenile whorls start to fade.

Juvenile shell

Adult coloration and ridging begin to appear.

*Lip is always fine in young shells*

At each new whorl of the spiral, the mollusk pauses to thicken its aperture (opening).

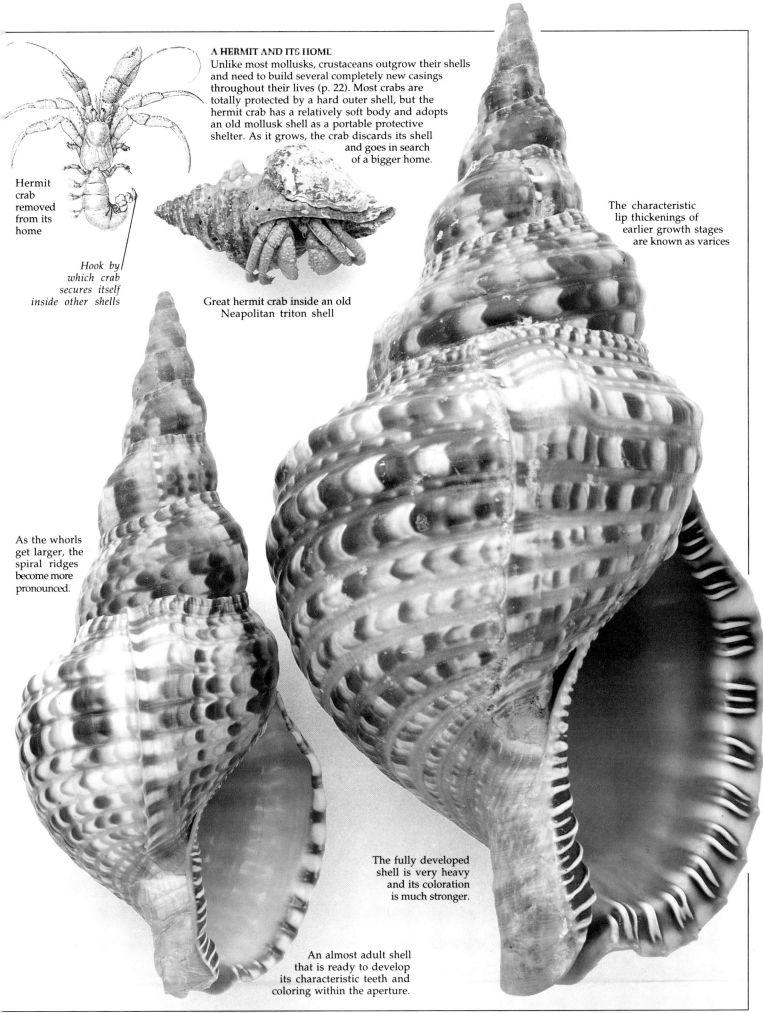

## A HERMIT AND ITS HOME

Unlike most mollusks, crustaceans outgrow their shells and need to build several completely new casings throughout their lives (p. 22). Most crabs are totally protected by a hard outer shell, but the hermit crab has a relatively soft body and adopts an old mollusk shell as a portable protective shelter. As it grows, the crab discards its shell and goes in search of a bigger home.

Hermit crab removed from its home

*Hook by which crab secures itself inside other shells*

Great hermit crab inside an old Neapolitan triton shell

The characteristic lip thickenings of earlier growth stages are known as varices

As the whorls get larger, the spiral ridges become more pronounced.

The fully developed shell is very heavy and its coloration is much stronger.

An almost adult shell that is ready to develop its characteristic teeth and coloring within the aperture.

# Shells for food lovers

As A FOOD RESOURCE, the sea offers an incredibly varied menu. In addition to fish, lobsters, and crabs, sea urchins and most mollusks are eaten all around the world. Many people who live near the sea survive almost entirely on seafood, and it is true that these are often the healthiest people - most seafood being rich in protein but low in calories. It is rather strange that many people shy away from the French delicacy of snails, but are quite happy to eat squid or a plate of spaghetti marinara, filled with small clams. Bivalve shells are the most popular form of shellfish; varieties of oyster, clam, scallop, cockle, and mussel are found in many parts of the world, and several types are farmed solely for human consumption. Some gastropods are also very popular; the abalone is sometimes eaten as steaks in parts of North America, Japan, and Australia, as is the queen conch throughout the Caribbean. In Europe, the whelk, a marine snail, is often fished commercially. For the shell collector, the fish market is often the best place to find local shells, especially in tropical areas.

**THE WALRUS AND THE CARPENTER**
In the Lewis Carroll story *Through the Looking-Glass,* the Walrus and the Carpenter ask some young oysters to take a stroll along the beach, and then proceed to eat the oysters with bread and butter!

*Hinge ligament*

**THE POPULAR CLAM**
Often used in soups and sauces, this small but abundant clam is found in great quantities in the seas of northern Europe. Its American cousin, a much larger but otherwise very similar bivalve called the Atlantic surf clam, is a major food source; some 45 million lbs (20 million kg) of its meat are fished each year between Nova Scotia and North Carolina.

**OYSTER CATCHER**
With its long, sharp beak, the oyster catcher is well equipped for digging bivalves from the sand.

**"ALIVE, ALIVE-O"**
Among the most popular of all edible mollusks is the oyster - each ocean has its own varieties, some more than double the size of these live Portuguese oysters. The traditional method of eating oysters is to swallow them whole, straight from the shell, uncooked and complete with all the natural juices. In times past, it was not uncommon to see street vendors serving live oysters to be eaten on the spot.

*Mantle tissue*

*Adductor muscle tissue*

Fresh oysters being sold in a street market

Portuguese oysters

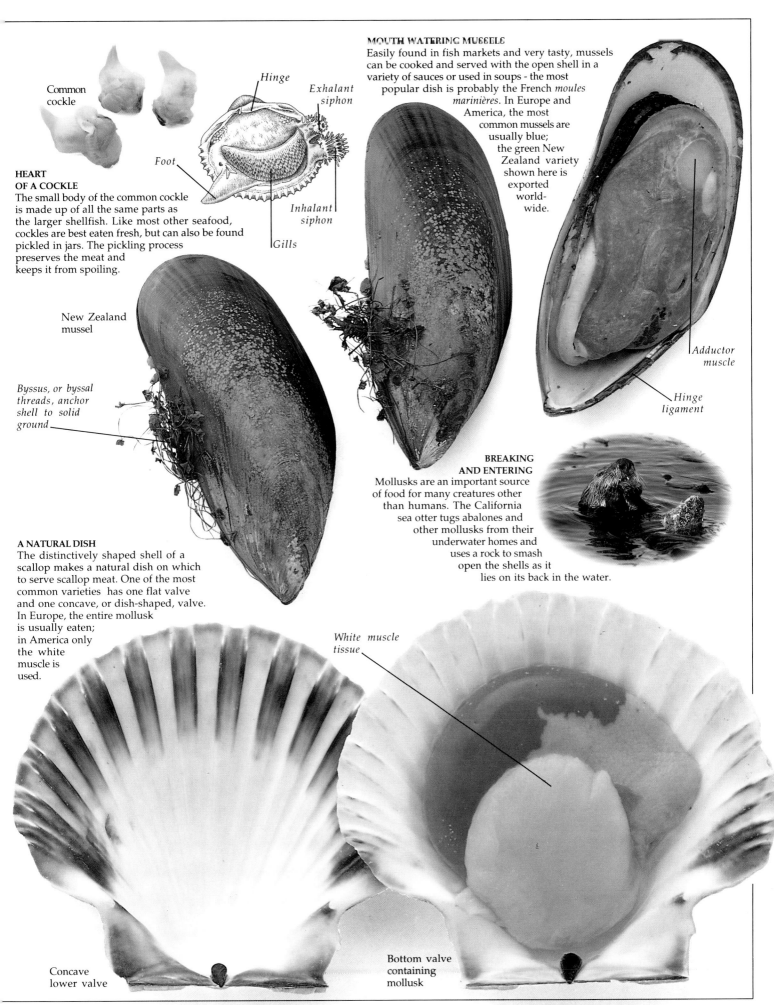

Common
cockle

*Hinge*

*Exhalant
siphon*

*Foot*

*Inhalant
siphon*

*Gills*

**HEART
OF A COCKLE**
The small body of the common cockle
is made up of all the same parts as
the larger shellfish. Like most other seafood,
cockles are best eaten fresh, but can also be found
pickled in jars. The pickling process
preserves the meat and
keeps it from spoiling.

**MOUTH WATERING MUSSELS**
Easily found in fish markets and very tasty, mussels
can be cooked and served with the open shell in a
variety of sauces or used in soups - the most
popular dish is probably the French *moules
marinières*. In Europe and
America, the most
common mussels are
usually blue;
the green New
Zealand variety
shown here is
exported
world-
wide.

New Zealand
mussel

*Byssus, or byssal
threads, anchor
shell to solid
ground*

*Adductor
muscle*

*Hinge
ligament*

**BREAKING
AND ENTERING**
Mollusks are an important source
of food for many creatures other
than humans. The California
sea otter tugs abalones and
other mollusks from their
underwater homes and
uses a rock to smash
open the shells as it
lies on its back in the water.

**A NATURAL DISH**
The distinctively shaped shell of a
scallop makes a natural dish on which
to serve scallop meat. One of the most
common varieties  has one flat valve
and one concave, or dish-shaped, valve.
In Europe, the entire mollusk
is usually eaten;
in America only
the white
muscle is
used.

*White muscle
tissue*

Concave
lower valve

Bottom valve
containing
mollusk

# A pearl is born

ALTHOUGH THEY ARE HIGHLY PRIZED by humans, pearls begin their lives as a nuisance to the creatures that make them. If a foreign body - such as a tiny piece of rock or the egg of a parasite - becomes lodged between the mantle of a mollusk and its shell, the animal will cover the object with layers of shelly material, or nacre, and create a pearl. In the case of pearl oyster shells, which have a rainbow-like interior, the pearls that are formed are as beautiful and lustrous as the inside of the shell. All types of mollusks are capable of producing pearls; bivalves are more likely to do so because they tend to live in a fixed position and are unable to extend out of their shells to dislodge a foreign body. Naturally formed pearls are extremely rare, but a way of cultivating pearls artificially was perfected by the Japanese at the start of this century, making cheaper pearls more accessible. By inserting an artificial nucleus into a living oyster, a good-size "cultured" pearl is virtually guaranteed after three to five years. The pearl industry is now so large that around 500 million pearls are produced each year.

**PEARLY BUDDHAS**

Although the Japanese are credited with perfecting the process of pearl cultivation, the Chinese had discovered pearlification - and put it to use - over 700 years before. Little clay figures of the god Buddha were inserted inside freshwater mussels and left for about a year, after which the shells would be opened to reveal perfectly coated mother-of-pearl figurines. Some mussels have been preserved with the tiny Buddhas still in place, but they were originally intended to be used as jewelry.

**BLISTERING BIVALVES**

A dome-shaped pearl that has developed while attached to the inside surface of an oyster shell is known as a blister pearl. These are quite common and are of little commercial value; they are generally used for decoration only. Very often the blisters reveal the nature of the object which is embedded against the shell, which may be a tiny crab or fish.

**PEARL OYSTER**

Even small oysters can produce reasonably large pearls, although the older and larger the shell, the greater the chance of finding a good-size pearl. This type of oyster grows to about 8 in (20 cm) and is common throughout the Indo-Pacific as well as the eastern Mediterranean, which it made its way to recently via the Suez Canal.

Freshwater pearls

**QUEEN MARY'S PEARLS**

Before the advent of cultured pearls, jewelry made with natural pearls was extremely expensive and therefore a symbol of great wealth or status. Queen Mary of England is remembered for the long strings of pearls she wore.

Nacre, or
mother-of-pearl

Blue pearls

Black-lipped
oyster

White pearls

Black pearls

Detail from a 17th-century
French engraving:
*Fishing for Pearls*

## PEARL FISHERS
Before the aqua-lung came into common use, pearl divers had to be extremely fit swimmers. In Japan, women known as *amas* still dive down to 40 ft (12 m) without air tanks to collect pearl oysters. Searching randomly for oysters that may contain pearls is very unproductive, as less than one in a thousand shells contains a good pearl.

## PEARLY KINGS AND QUEENS
The traditional "holiday garments" worn by East London street vendors consist of outfits covered in pearl buttons. The custom goes back to the Roman invasion of Britain, when some British natives wore shell costumes.

## VARIETY IN THE PEARL WORLD
Pearls come in all shapes and sizes: the largest in the world is 1.5 in (38 mm) in diameter. The shape of a pearl is also quite variable and, while perfectly round pearls are the most popular, some may be tear-shaped and others irregular. Blue, black and even yellow forms of pearl exist and, because they are scarcer than the white forms, they are more highly prized. The colour depends on the nature of the shell in which the pearls are formed and the pigments secreted in the nacre.

Pearl

## DOG COCKLE PEARLS
Although not as attractive as an oyster pearl, and therefore less valuable, this pearl inside a European dog cockle is a lot rarer. Some pearls that come from shells other than oysters may be very valuable - the Caribbean conch shell, for example, produces pink pearls, the necklaces of which can cost thousands of dollars.

# Fossil finds

Fossilized sand dollar from Florida

WE ARE LUCKY IN THAT it is quite easy to trace the history of shelled animals back through many millions of years. The soft parts of an animal will rot away quickly after it dies, but the shells are preserved for long periods of time and can often be found as fossils (remains of the empty shell that have been turned into rock over millions of years, or identical casts of the long-gone shell). Fossil evidence shows how certain species have changed with the passage of time; in many cases animals have had to evolve in order to cope with changes in their environment, such as a change in temperature or in the sources of food available. Some animals have remained unchanged, presumably because they are in perfect harmony with their environment.

*Tentacled head would have emerged from here.*

**Fossilized ammonites from Dorset, England**

Curled-up fossil trilobites

Uncurled trilobite

"Snakestone" ammonite forgery

**FOSSIL FORGERY**
Among the best-known fossils are those of the ammonites, which became extinct over 140 million years ago. The ammonites were a form of cephalopod (p. 8), related to the nautilus still living today. In Whitby, England, the fossils were once thought to represent coiled serpents that had been beheaded and turned to stone by the Saxon abbess St. Hilda. In order to maintain this legend, snakes' heads were commonly carved on fossil ammonites sold to tourists in the area.

**TALE OF THE TRILOBITES**
The trilobites were another common animal that became extinct some 248 million years ago. These were primitive marine creatures related to the crustaceans that abound in our seas today. Like lobsters and crabs, trilobites had the ability to shed their plated skin, so trilobite fossils are fairly common. Some are found curled up, like a modern wood louse, for protection. There were thousands of species of trilobite - the largest type measuring some 28 in (70 cm) long.

Impression of trilobite embedded in rock

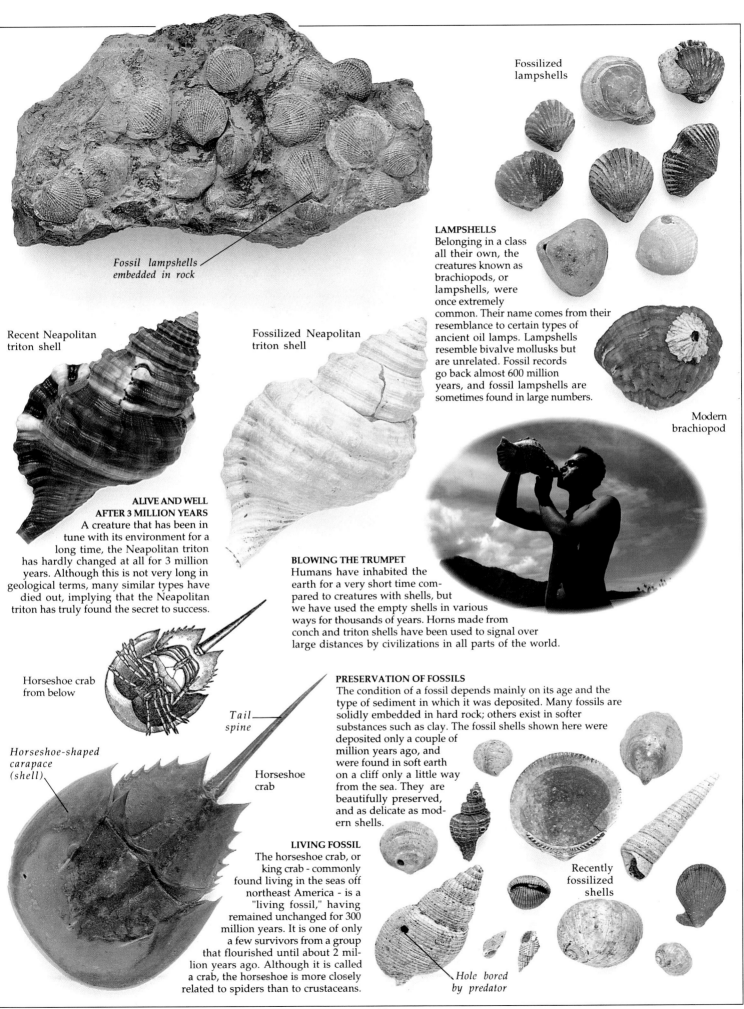

Fossilized
lampshells

Fossil lampshells
embedded in rock

**LAMPSHELLS**
Belonging in a class
all their own, the
creatures known as
brachiopods, or
lampshells, were
once extremely
common. Their name comes from their
resemblance to certain types of
ancient oil lamps. Lampshells
resemble bivalve mollusks but
are unrelated. Fossil records
go back almost 600 million
years, and fossil lampshells are
sometimes found in large numbers.

Modern
brachiopod

Recent Neapolitan
triton shell

Fossilized Neapolitan
triton shell

**ALIVE AND WELL
AFTER 3 MILLION YEARS**
A creature that has been in
tune with its environment for a
long time, the Neapolitan triton
has hardly changed at all for 3 million
years. Although this is not very long in
geological terms, many similar types have
died out, implying that the Neapolitan
triton has truly found the secret to success.

**BLOWING THE TRUMPET**
Humans have inhabited the
earth for a very short time compared to creatures with shells, but
we have used the empty shells in various
ways for thousands of years. Horns made from
conch and triton shells have been used to signal over
large distances by civilizations in all parts of the world.

Horseshoe crab
from below

Tail
spine

**PRESERVATION OF FOSSILS**
The condition of a fossil depends mainly on its age and the
type of sediment in which it was deposited. Many fossils are
solidly embedded in hard rock; others exist in softer
substances such as clay. The fossil shells shown here were
deposited only a couple of
million years ago, and
were found in soft earth
on a cliff only a little way
from the sea. They are
beautifully preserved,
and as delicate as mod-
ern shells.

Horseshoe-shaped
carapace
(shell)

Horseshoe
crab

**LIVING FOSSIL**
The horseshoe crab, or
king crab - commonly
found living in the seas off
northeast America - is a
"living fossil," having
remained unchanged for 300
million years. It is one of only
a few survivors from a group
that flourished until about 2 million years ago. Although it is called
a crab, the horseshoe is more closely
related to spiders than to crustaceans.

Recently
fossilized
shells

Hole bored
by predator

39

# Cases for places

IN THE WORLD OF NATURE, being seen or not seen can be the difference between life and death. As creatures move into new environments, or their environment changes, those best suited are the ones that survive. They go through gradual changes, often over millions of years, that permit them to continue to live quite peacefully. Sometimes these are simply changes in habits; but in other cases, creatures evolve the art of camouflage - the ability to blend in with the background and stay unnoticed by predators in their chosen habitats. In the shell world, creatures have many ways of protecting themselves: there are crabs that cover themselves with algae, and mollusks that permanently secure loose objects to their shells. Color also plays an important part in camouflage, and there are many shells that are perfectly designed to blend in with their surroundings. Some mollusks can actually change color almost instantly, like chameleons. Finally, there are some shells that simply allow themselves to be covered by plant growth, barnacles, or even deposits of lime.

**CHAMELEON PRAWN**
Cleverly concealed in a sea lettuce, this prawn changes color to match the color of the seaweed on which it is living. At night, however, it always turns a transparent blue color.

Carrier shell
with pebbles

Piece of glass
bottle attached
to carrier shell

Coral on which
Babel's latiaxis
lives

Latiaxis encrusted
with marine
growth

Underside of
carrier shell
and aperture
(opening)

Aperture
(opening)
side of
coated
shell

Cleaned
shell

**WELCOME ATTACHMENTS**
Although barnacles can be a nuisance when stuck to ships, they are useful as camouflage for the shore crab (above). If the crab keeps still, it looks more like a stone than a living creature.

**SHELL COLLECTORS**
Carrier shells are so-called because as they grow, some of them can attach a variety of objects to themselves, ranging from dead shells and coral, to pebbles, and sometimes even bits of garbage left by humans. They live mainly in deep water in most of the world's warm seas.

**LIME COATINGS**
When alive, most shells are crusted with marine plants and animals that make them difficult to find underwater. Sometimes deposits can cover a shell entirely. Divers often have trouble locating latiaxis shells (left). They live on coral, and are often so well disguised that the divers have to feel along the coral surface for the shells with their hands.

# Snail in the grass

The color varieties within land snail shells often seem infinite. The common European banded snail displays enormous variety in its shell color and pattern, each designed to blend it in with its habitat and protect it from predators.

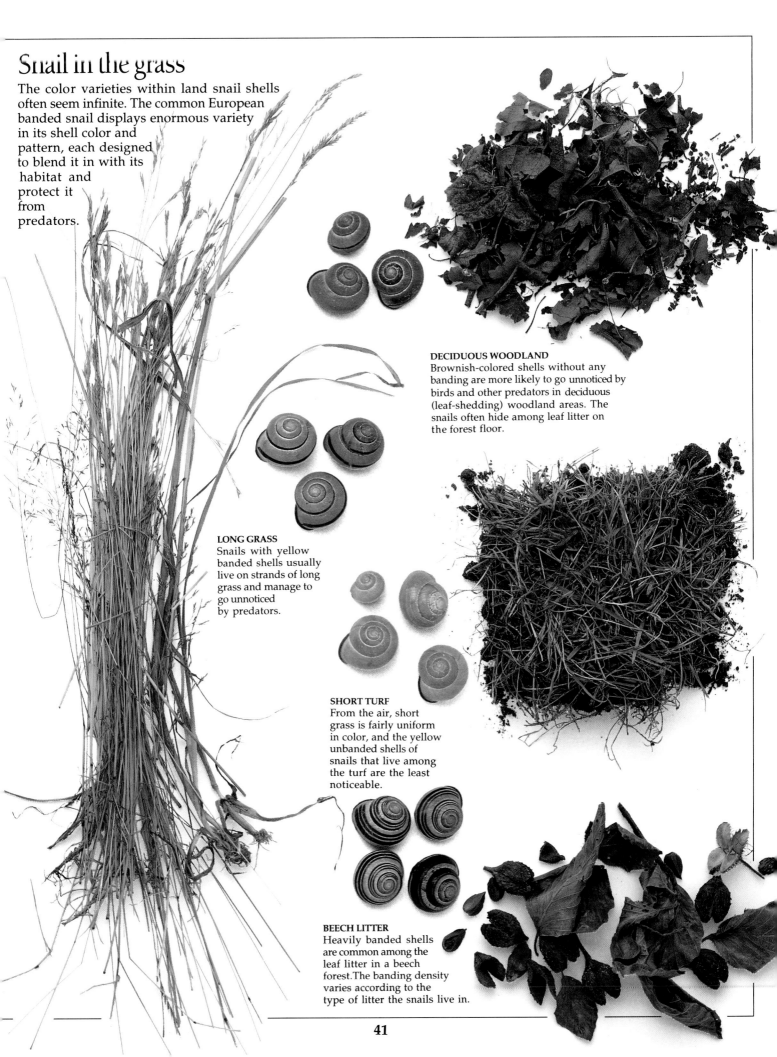

### DECIDUOUS WOODLAND
Brownish-colored shells without any banding are more likely to go unnoticed by birds and other predators in deciduous (leaf-shedding) woodland areas. The snails often hide among leaf litter on the forest floor.

### LONG GRASS
Snails with yellow banded shells usually live on strands of long grass and manage to go unnoticed by predators.

### SHORT TURF
From the air, short grass is fairly uniform in color, and the yellow unbanded shells of snails that live among the turf are the least noticeable.

### BEECH LITTER
Heavily banded shells are common among the leaf litter in a beech forest. The banding density varies according to the type of litter the snails live in.

41

# Settlers on the sands

Unless a rocky coastline or coral reef (pp. 46-53), a sandy shore seems to offer little shelter for shelled creatures. However, in order to avoid being exposed, many of the animals found on sandy shores are burrowers, sometimes spending their entire lives buried deep below the surface. When a sandy beach is exposed at low tide it seems a lifeless, apparently barren environment, but close inspection will reveal a variety of holes, mounds, and tracks - all evidence of animals that have dug down to where moisture is retained until the next tide. Sometimes hundreds of shells may be living in an area of sand no larger than this page.

Necklace shells

**Saint James's scallop**

**FLAT-SIDE-UP**
Scallops are a popular food (p. 35), and the scallop shell is the symbol of Saint James, the fisherman. The two valves of Saint James's scallop are very different in shape: the bottom valve, commonly put to use as an ashtray, is domed, and the top valve is flattened. The scallops lie with their bottom valve buried in the sand.

## NECKLACE SHELLS
Necklace shells are so-called because they lay their eggs in coiled, straplike bands. These gastropod mollusks are common predators that plow through the sand in search of food. They drill circular holes in bivalve shells and eat the animals inside.

## SUNDIAL SHELLS
These gastropods, also known as architect shells, have elegant spiral shells and are found on tropical sandy shores. Some sundial shells measure just a few millimeters in diameter and live in very deep water.

Tropical sundials

**SANDY EXPANSES**
The long stretches of sandy beach that occur on many coasts are formed by waves, tides, and currents. Sea cliffs are eroded by waves and weather, and the rock, mixed with shells, is broken into tiny particles. This mixture eventually ends up as sand; onshore as a beach, and offshore as a sandbar or bank.

## MARGIN SHELLS
These colorful shells can be found on the sandy shores of many warm countries. Empty specimens that wash up on the beach do not usually have the naturally polished look of living shells.

West African margin shells

## SPOTTED DIGGERS
Eloise's acteon

These colorful acteon shells burrow into the sand with their flattened, spadelike heads. Acteon shells can be found in many of the world's seas; these two are of a type only recently discovered in the Persian Gulf.

## BUBBLES AND CANOES
Bubble and canoe shells are closely related mollusks that occur in a variety of marine environments. They slide along the surface of fine mud in search of small mollusks, which they eat by crushing them with their powerful gizzards (stomachs). The animals are often many times larger than their fragile, inflated shells.

Bubble shell

Canoe bubble shell

## BURROWING BIVALVES
The majority of shells found on sandy shores are bivalves. The Mediterranean scraper solecurtus and the Indo-Pacific sunset siliqua (both also known as razor clams) are typical of bivalve shells that use their muscles to pull themselves deep into the sand when the tide goes out.

Sunset siliqua

Scraper solecurtus

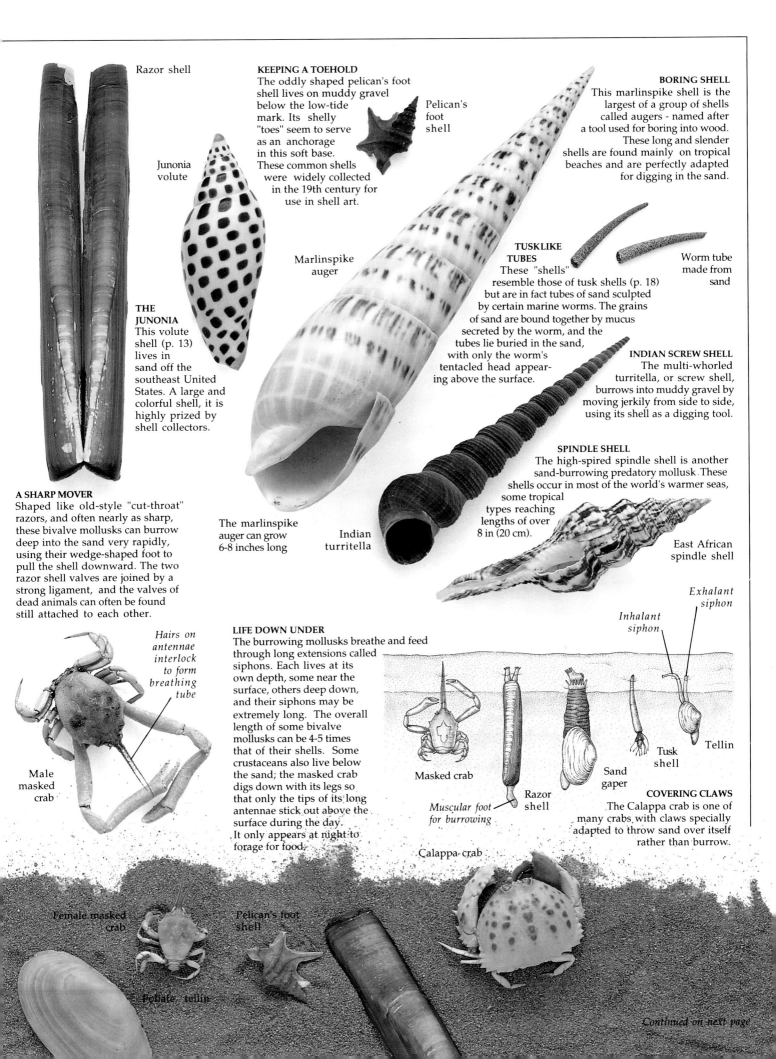

Razor shell

Junonia volute

**KEEPING A TOEHOLD**
The oddly shaped pelican's foot shell lives on muddy gravel below the low-tide mark. Its shelly "toes" seem to serve as an anchorage in this soft base. These common shells were widely collected in the 19th century for use in shell art.

Pelican's foot shell

**BORING SHELL**
This marlinspike shell is the largest of a group of shells called augers - named after a tool used for boring into wood. These long and slender shells are found mainly on tropical beaches and are perfectly adapted for digging in the sand.

Marlinspike auger

**THE JUNONIA**
This volute shell (p. 13) lives in sand off the southeast United States. A large and colorful shell, it is highly prized by shell collectors.

**TUSKLIKE TUBES**
These "shells" resemble those of tusk shells (p. 18) but are in fact tubes of sand sculpted by certain marine worms. The grains of sand are bound together by mucus secreted by the worm, and the tubes lie buried in the sand, with only the worm's tentacled head appearing above the surface.

Worm tube made from sand

**INDIAN SCREW SHELL**
The multi-whorled turritella, or screw shell, burrows into muddy gravel by moving jerkily from side to side, using its shell as a digging tool.

**A SHARP MOVER**
Shaped like old-style "cut-throat" razors, and often nearly as sharp, these bivalve mollusks can burrow deep into the sand very rapidly, using their wedge-shaped foot to pull the shell downward. The two razor shell valves are joined by a strong ligament, and the valves of dead animals can often be found still attached to each other.

The marlinspike auger can grow 6-8 inches long

Indian turritella

**SPINDLE SHELL**
The high-spired spindle shell is another sand-burrowing predatory mollusk. These shells occur in most of the world's warmer seas, some tropical types reaching lengths of over 8 in (20 cm).

East African spindle shell

Hairs on antennae interlock to form breathing tube

**LIFE DOWN UNDER**
The burrowing mollusks breathe and feed through long extensions called siphons. Each lives at its own depth, some near the surface, others deep down, and their siphons may be extremely long. The overall length of some bivalve mollusks can be 4-5 times that of their shells. Some crustaceans also live below the sand; the masked crab digs down with its legs so that only the tips of its long antennae stick out above the surface during the day. It only appears at night to forage for food.

Exhalant siphon

Inhalant siphon

Male masked crab

Masked crab

Muscular foot for burrowing

Razor shell

Sand gaper

Tusk shell

Tellin

**COVERING CLAWS**
The Calappa crab is one of many crabs with claws specially adapted to throw sand over itself rather than burrow.

Calappa crab

Female masked crab

Pelican's foot shell

Foliate tellin

*Continued on next page*

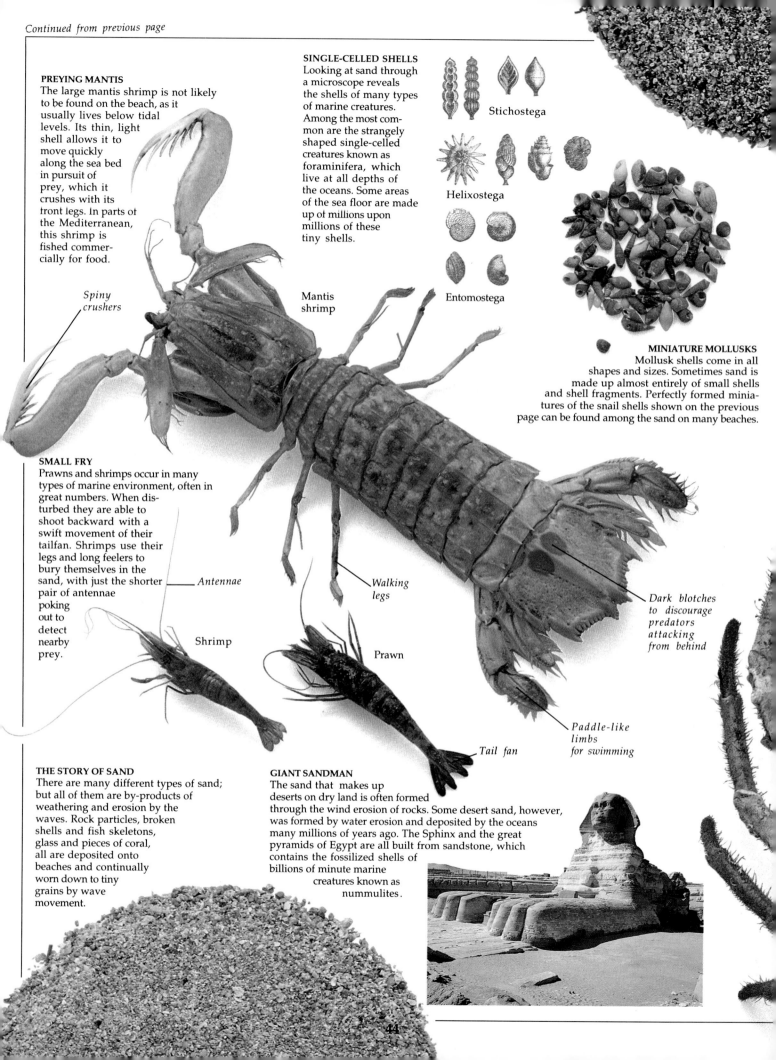

### PREYING MANTIS
The large mantis shrimp is not likely to be found on the beach, as it usually lives below tidal levels. Its thin, light shell allows it to move quickly along the sea bed in pursuit of prey, which it crushes with its front legs. In parts of the Mediterranean, this shrimp is fished commercially for food.

*Spiny crushers*

### SINGLE-CELLED SHELLS
Looking at sand through a microscope reveals the shells of many types of marine creatures. Among the most common are the strangely shaped single-celled creatures known as foraminifera, which live at all depths of the oceans. Some areas of the sea floor are made up of millions upon millions of these tiny shells.

Stichostega

Helixostega

Entomostega

Mantis shrimp

### MINIATURE MOLLUSKS
Mollusk shells come in all shapes and sizes. Sometimes sand is made up almost entirely of small shells and shell fragments. Perfectly formed miniatures of the snail shells shown on the previous page can be found among the sand on many beaches.

### SMALL FRY
Prawns and shrimps occur in many types of marine environment, often in great numbers. When disturbed they are able to shoot backward with a swift movement of their tailfan. Shrimps use their legs and long feelers to bury themselves in the sand, with just the shorter pair of antennae poking out to detect nearby prey.

*Antennae*

Shrimp

*Walking legs*

Prawn

*Dark blotches to discourage predators attacking from behind*

*Paddle-like limbs for swimming*

*Tail fan*

### THE STORY OF SAND
There are many different types of sand; but all of them are by-products of weathering and erosion by the waves. Rock particles, broken shells and fish skeletons, glass and pieces of coral, all are deposited onto beaches and continually worn down to tiny grains by wave movement.

### GIANT SANDMAN
The sand that makes up deserts on dry land is often formed through the wind erosion of rocks. Some desert sand, however, was formed by water erosion and deposited by the oceans many millions of years ago. The Sphinx and the great pyramids of Egypt are all built from sandstone, which contains the fossilized shells of billions of minute marine creatures known as nummulites.

44

Sand made
up of small
shells and tiny
shell fragments

Sand dollar
with spines

Swimming
crab

**SWIMMING CRAB**
Some of the crabs living on
sandy shores have adapted
their fifth pair of legs for
swimming rather than
walking, the last joint
being shaped like a
rounded, flat paddle.

*Swimming
paddles*

Caribbean
sea biscuit

Philippine
sand
dollar

*Long pincer for
catching prey in
deep crevices*

Spiny spider
crab

**STAYING
POWER**
Sea urchins, which
include sand dollars and sea
biscuits, are typical inhabitants of
sandy shores in warmer areas, especially Caribbean and Australian
waters. The living sand dollar is
covered in hundreds of tiny spines and
lives just below the surface of the
sand. Its flattened shape permits the
sand dollar to stay in the same spot
as water flows smoothly over.

*Barnacles and
worm tubes
attached to
carapace*

*Walking
legs*

**THORNS IN THE SAND**
The spiny spider crab is easily
recognizable by its small spiny
body and long legs. Its carapace
(shell) is often encrusted with other
marine organisms, and young crabs are
known to cover themselves with seaweeds
and algae for camouflage. They live on the
lower shore and gather to breed in the summer,
forming heaps of up to 80 crabs. Because of
their spiny carapaces, these crabs are also
known as thornbacks. Fishermen searching for thornbacks submerged in the sand
walk the beaches barefoot and
feel for the crabs with their feet.

# Life on the rocks

ROCKY SHORES provide a diverse and complex environment for many types of marine creatures. The types of rock from which a beach is made, its position in relation to the sea, and the range of tide levels all play a part in determining the variety of creatures that live there. Where the tide exposes the rocky shore for several hours each day, some creatures have built up a tolerance to living without water for extended periods. Those that have not managed to reach deeper waters or find tidal pools when the water recedes, will dry out and die from exposure to the air and sun. These are not the only elements to which a rocky shore may be exposed; the pounding of powerful waves erodes the rocks themselves. Many animals living on the rocks have evolved very strong shells that can withstand the force of the waves, and many have developed ways of anchoring themselves firmly to the surface of the rocks, so they are not washed away. The rocky sea bed plays host to an even wider range of creatures, many of which spend much of their lives hidden in holes or underneath rocks.

### ROCK-POOL INHABITANTS
Life can be hard in the shallow water pools left by receding tides. Many creatures that prefer less light and warmth are left stranded and must try their best to find shelter.

Bearded ark shell

### BOUVIER'S CRAB
Like many small crabs, this one lives between or under rocks, and only emerges to scavenge for food at night.

### BEARDED ARK SHELL
So-called because of the tiny hairs that cover its shell, this is a bivalve that lives in rock crevices, attaching itself by means of a broad byssus (left). The shell of this creature is often distorted as it grows to fit snugly in its rocky recess.

New Zealand mussel

Mussel with byssal threads

*Tail fan*

### MUSSELS WITH ANCHORS
Mussels are common inhabitants of many rocky coasts, often living in massive clusters high on the shore. Mussels anchor themselves to rocks and other surfaces by means of byssal threads - strong, thin filaments planted by the mussel's foot.

Common blue mussels

**THE JEWEL IN THE SHELL**
This rough star shell lives on the rocky shores of the Mediterranean, but is found below tide level. The shell is often heavily encrusted with marine growths. The bright-red operculum is sometimes used to make jewelry.

*Operculum*

**WINKLES ON THE WEEDS**
The tiny periwinkles are among the most common inhabitants of rocky shores. These snails live high up on the shore, clinging to rocks and clumps of seaweed.

Rough periwinkles

*Antenna*

*Claw*

*Common shore crab*

**COMMON CRAB**
The shore crab is one of the most common European crabs, and can be found lurking under rocks and seaweed.

**ELUSIVE LOBSTER**
The common lobster is highly prized for food and is a favorite catch for divers. Lobsters can be difficult to find, as they blend in with their surroundings and often hide away in crevices during the day, with only their claws and antennae showing.

**STONY-SHELLED CRAB**
The Mediterranean stone crab is so-called because of its heavy-looking, irregular shell.

*Walking legs*

Holes for
expulsion of
water and
waste

**COLORFUL EAR SHELLS**
Abalones, or ormers, like this California
green abalone, are also known as ear
shells because of their shape. The
row of holes in the shell allows
water and waste to be passed
out. The animals inside are
eaten in many parts of the
world, and the shells
are used to make
jewelry.

Lamellose
ormer

Chiton shells
(see p. 18)

**BARNACLE ROCK SHELL**
This odd-looking shell,
found off the coasts of Peru
and Chile, is related to the
murex shells (p. 12), but sits on
rocks, much like a limpet
(below).

**LONG-LASTING LIMPETS**
Limpets are well known for
holding on tight to rocks
so as not to be knocked
off by strong waves.
A magnetic mine that
clings to ships' hulls
has been named
after them.
Limpet shells are
usually either very
eroded or covered
with algae and other
forms of marine life.

Barnacles
and algae on
limpet shell

Safian
limpet
shell

**KILLER SNAILS**
Most rocky shores play host
to snails that feed on
bivalves such as mus-
sels and oysters. Some
"drill" into the shells
of their prey;
others, like the Pana-
manian thorn latirus,
have developed a special
tooth that helps to break
open the shells.

Thorn
latirus

Tooth

Sting
winkle

European
china
limpet

48

# Rock-boring shells

Some shelled creatures have overcome the problem of being washed away by strong waves by sticking to rocks permanently, or even boring into them. These animals feed by extending tubes or fans out from their shells to catch prey, or by opening their valves and allowing the current to bring microscopic food to them. The creatures that hide away in holes in the rocks are not only safe from being washed away, but are also protected from most of their enemies.

**BURROWING SEA URCHINS**
Certain types of sea urchin use their spines to dig out holes in sand, mud, or rocks. This protects them from the force of waves or currents. They hold on to the rock with their rows of suckered tube feet.

*Limestone*    *Shell*

**READY-MADE HOMES**
Retzius shells settle in holes that already exist in rocks, but the animal enlarges its home as it grows. Eventually, it becomes firmly wedged in, making it impossible for the shell to be dislodged by the waves.

*Calcareous tube*

**GIVE-AWAY TUBE**
Some of the creatures that live inside rocks are only visible because of a shelly tube, which they extend from their hidden home.

*Top valve of shell*

**STUCK LIKE GLUE**
The jewel box shell is a bivalve that does not live inside the rock but cements its lower valve to the surface in the same way as some types of oyster.

**DIGGING DOWN DEEP**
The piddock shell can be found buried in a variety of hard substances, which it bores into mechanically with its two valves. Some types of piddock can live up to 3 ft (1 m) below the surface.

*Piddock hole in rock*

Date mussel removed from rock

*Piddock shell and siphon*

*Shell embedded in rock*

Piddock shell removed from rock

**ROCK EROSION**
Unlike the piddock, date mussels do not use their valves to bore holes. Instead they secrete a special chemical that softens the rock. Then the rock is scraped away and flushed out by water currents from the mussel's siphons. Date mussels are edible.

**BLISTERING BARNACLES**
Barnacles often cling to rocky shorelines in massive colonies. They also attach themselves to the undersides of boats, and have to be scraped off so they don't slow the boat down.

**WHERE'S THE WORM?**
Although commonly called worm shells, these irregularly shaped tubes belong to gastropod mollusks, which spend their lives cemented to hard surfaces.

*Worm tubes on thorny oyster*

**SHELLS UPON SHELLS**
Shells that spend their lives stuck to one spot frequently provide suitable homes for other shells. White shelly tubes belonging to a certain type of marine worm are often seen on rocks and other shells.

Cluster of barnacles

*Worm shells on rock*

*Worm tubes on Mediterranean blue mussel shell*

# Residents of the reefs

CORAL REEFS ARE COMPLEX NETWORKS of millions of living organisms, supporting more life than any other type of marine environment. They are like underwater gardens, with a wide variety of different colors and textures, and very dependent on sunlight and warmth for survival. Most coral occurs in warm regions of the world; many large coral outcrops are found in the Caribbean, off West Africa, and throughout the Indo-Pacific. Some outcrops are huge, the most famous being Australia's Great Barrier Reef, which stretches for over 1,250 miles (2,000 km). Among the multitude of animals inhabiting the reefs are many shelled creatures, although they may be difficult to spot because they hide under between the corals during the day. Not until the relative safety of darkness do they emerge in search of food. The shallow-water reefs and the life they support are extremely vulnerable, and although many coral reefs were established long before humans existed on earth, they are being threatened by pollution and over-eager collectors.

**LEGENDS OF THE REEFS**
Mermaids and sea nymphs are legendary creatures thought by ancient sailors to inhabit the seas around coral reefs. They are often shown as using the spiny shell of a murex to comb their long hair.

Violet coral shell

**VIOLET CORAL SHELL**
This little shell is a typical inhabitant of tropical reefs, usually living in crevices or hollows of live coral heads. Females of this species are often larger than males.

Princely cone

Marble cone

Papal miter

Fluted growth layers

**FLUTED FILTER FEEDER**
A smaller relative of the giant clam (p. 17), which grows to over 5 ft (1.5 m) in length, this pretty clam can be found on shallow reefs through-out most of the Indo-Pacific area. It is a filter feeder - it lies with its valves apart and sifts the tiny plants and animals from the water.

**CONES AND MITERS**
Some of the largest and most decorative mollusk shells of the coral reefs are the cone and miter shells. Although they belong to different families, both shells are prized for their bright colors and pat-terns. Cone shells are also famous for their ability to shoot a paralyzing·dart into their prey. This has killed some shell collectors.

**COLORFUL COWRIES**
Among the prettiest and most diverse creatures to be found on the reefs are the popular cowrie shells. The smaller types are often live on the underside of coral slabs.

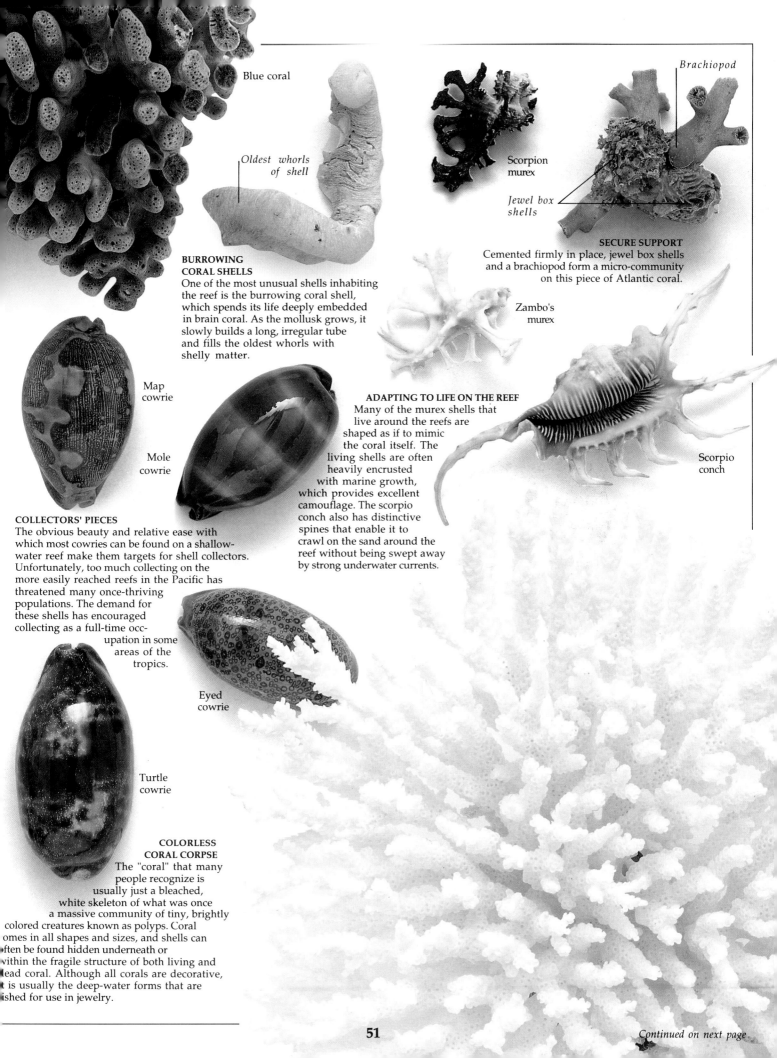

Blue coral

*Oldest whorls of shell*

Scorpion murex

*Brachiopod*

*Jewel box shells*

**SECURE SUPPORT**
Cemented firmly in place, jewel box shells
and a brachiopod form a micro-community
on this piece of Atlantic coral.

Zambo's murex

## BURROWING CORAL SHELLS

One of the most unusual shells inhabiting
the reef is the burrowing coral shell,
which spends its life deeply embedded
in brain coral. As the mollusk grows, it
slowly builds a long, irregular tube
and fills the oldest whorls with
shelly matter.

Map cowrie

Mole cowrie

## ADAPTING TO LIFE ON THE REEF

Many of the murex shells that
live around the reefs are
shaped as if to mimic
the coral itself. The
living shells are often
heavily encrusted
with marine growth,
which provides excellent
camouflage. The scorpio
conch also has distinctive
spines that enable it to
crawl on the sand around the
reef without being swept away
by strong underwater currents.

Scorpio conch

## COLLECTORS' PIECES

The obvious beauty and relative ease with
which most cowries can be found on a shallow-
water reef make them targets for shell collectors.
Unfortunately, too much collecting on the
more easily reached reefs in the Pacific has
threatened many once-thriving
populations. The demand for
these shells has encouraged
collecting as a full-time occ-
upation in some
areas of the
tropics.

Eyed cowrie

Turtle cowrie

## COLORLESS CORAL CORPSE

The "coral" that many
people recognize is
usually just a bleached,
white skeleton of what was once
a massive community of tiny, brightly
colored creatures known as polyps. Coral
comes in all shapes and sizes, and shells can
often be found hidden underneath or
within the fragile structure of both living and
dead coral. Although all corals are decorative,
it is usually the deep-water forms that are
fished for use in jewelry.

*Continued on next page*

**BORN OF THE OCEAN**
Rising out of the sea, Erskine Island off Queensland, Australia, is made from dead coral and surrounded by living coral. Thousands of tiny coral islands like this one can be found on Australia's Great Barrier Reef.

Color range in tests of tropical sea urchins

**TROPICAL TURTLES**
Marine turtles can sometimes be seen in the warm waters surrounding tropical coral reefs. The hawksbill turtle (p. 31) is a typical coral-reef dweller. Because of the abundance of marine life, shallow-water reefs are ideal feeding grounds for many types of creature. Some marine turtles have developed incredible migratory habits, traveling hundreds of miles from their feeding grounds to nest on the beaches where they were born. The green turtle (below) travels to its nesting ground every two or three years.

Green turtle

**SPINY REEF DWELLERS**
Common inhabitants of most coral reefs are the sea urchins (p. 20). Their spine-covered tests are usually found in reef hollows. The sea urchins are mainly herbivorous (plant eating), feeding on tiny algae scraped off rock and dead coral.

**CARNIVOROUS PLANT?**
These strange-looking specimens may look like plants, but are in fact polyps. This straw tubularia is a carnivorous (meat eating) polyp with long stems encased in yellowish tubes. These creatures attach themselves readily to shells and stones.

*Smooth laminae (bony plates) do not overlap*

Color of shell can be green, brown or black

Skeleton of
brain coral

**BRAIN OR MUSHROOM?**
Two of the most common types of coral found in
tropical areas are brain corals and mushroom corals.
From the pictures, it is not difficult to see why they
got their names! Brain corals, made by a colony
containing millions of tiny coral polyps, grow into a
heap with patterning like the folds found on brains.
The smaller mushroom corals are disklike, look
almost edible, and because they are not attached to a
hard base, can move short distances.

Skeleton of
mushroom
coral

Living brain
coral in front
of sea fan

# Crustaceans and corals

The crustaceans have successfully made homes for
themselves in coral reefs, as they have in all marine
environments. Crabs, lobsters, and shrimps can be
found there in great variety. Some,
such as the coral-gall crab (below),
actually live inside the coral; others
display bright colors or unusual
shapes that help them to blend in
with the coral garden.

**CORAL-DWELLING CRAB**
The coral-gall crab settles on coral
when very young and becomes en-
veloped as the coral grows.

**A LIVING PEARL**
With its knobby shell, the
tropical spotted rock crab, or
pearl crab (below), is easily
recognizable.

Galls on the living coral

**NOW YOU
SEE IT...**
The ghost crab is so-called because it is the same color as the
sandy tropical beaches where it
lives, and seems to appear and
disappear at random.

# Deep-sea dwellers

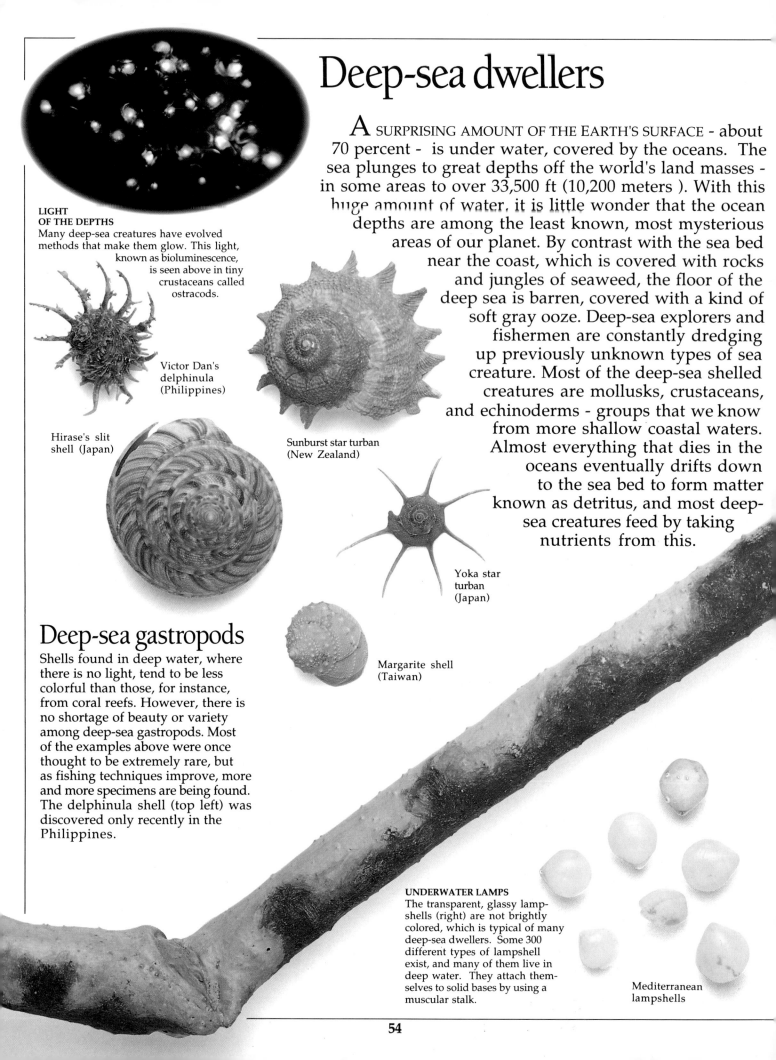

A SURPRISING AMOUNT OF THE EARTH'S SURFACE - about 70 percent - is under water, covered by the oceans. The sea plunges to great depths off the world's land masses - in some areas to over 33,500 ft (10,200 meters ). With this huge amount of water, it is little wonder that the ocean depths are among the least known, most mysterious areas of our planet. By contrast with the sea bed near the coast, which is covered with rocks and jungles of seaweed, the floor of the deep sea is barren, covered with a kind of soft gray ooze. Deep-sea explorers and fishermen are constantly dredging up previously unknown types of sea creature. Most of the deep-sea shelled creatures are mollusks, crustaceans, and echinoderms - groups that we know from more shallow coastal waters. Almost everything that dies in the oceans eventually drifts down to the sea bed to form matter known as detritus, and most deep-sea creatures feed by taking nutrients from this.

**LIGHT OF THE DEPTHS**
Many deep-sea creatures have evolved methods that make them glow. This light, known as bioluminescence, is seen above in tiny crustaceans called ostracods.

Victor Dan's delphinula (Philippines)

Hirase's slit shell (Japan)

Sunburst star turban (New Zealand)

Yoka star turban (Japan)

Margarite shell (Taiwan)

## Deep-sea gastropods

Shells found in deep water, where there is no light, tend to be less colorful than those, for instance, from coral reefs. However, there is no shortage of beauty or variety among deep-sea gastropods. Most of the examples above were once thought to be extremely rare, but as fishing techniques improve, more and more specimens are being found. The delphinula shell (top left) was discovered only recently in the Philippines.

**UNDERWATER LAMPS**
The transparent, glassy lamp-shells (right) are not brightly colored, which is typical of many deep-sea dwellers. Some 300 different types of lampshell exist, and many of them live in deep water. They attach themselves to solid bases by using a muscular stalk.

Mediterranean lampshells

# Deep sea crustacea

Crustaceans are among the most abundant of creatures to be found in deep water. They range from tiny ostracods (left-hand page) to massive crabs, like the Japanese spider crab (leg shown below), and blind deep-sea lobsters whose fossils were known long before living examples were found. Some of the larger crustaceans are fished by laying traps, but most of them live a peaceful life in the darkness of the sea bed, out of human reach.

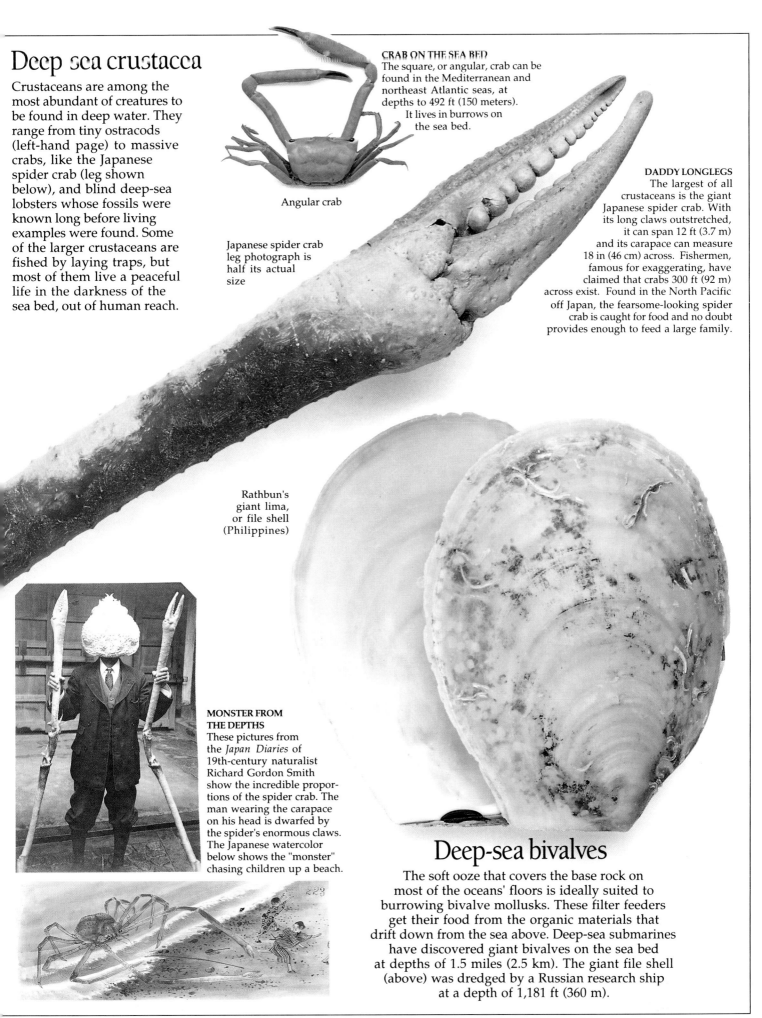

**CRAB ON THE SEA BED**
The square, or angular, crab can be found in the Mediterranean and northeast Atlantic seas, at depths to 492 ft (150 meters). It lives in burrows on the sea bed.

Angular crab

Japanese spider crab leg photograph is half its actual size

**DADDY LONGLEGS**
The largest of all crustaceans is the giant Japanese spider crab. With its long claws outstretched, it can span 12 ft (3.7 m) and its carapace can measure 18 in (46 cm) across. Fishermen, famous for exaggerating, have claimed that crabs 300 ft (92 m) across exist. Found in the North Pacific off Japan, the fearsome-looking spider crab is caught for food and no doubt provides enough to feed a large family.

Rathbun's giant lima, or file shell (Philippines)

**MONSTER FROM THE DEPTHS**
These pictures from the *Japan Diaries* of 19th-century naturalist Richard Gordon Smith show the incredible proportions of the spider crab. The man wearing the carapace on his head is dwarfed by the spider's enormous claws. The Japanese watercolor below shows the "monster" chasing children up a beach.

## Deep-sea bivalves

The soft ooze that covers the base rock on most of the oceans' floors is ideally suited to burrowing bivalve mollusks. These filter feeders get their food from the organic materials that drift down from the sea above. Deep-sea submarines have discovered giant bivalves on the sea bed at depths of 1.5 miles (2.5 km). The giant file shell (above) was dredged by a Russian research ship at a depth of 1,181 ft (360 m).

# Freshwater finds

T HE VARIETY OF LIFE in freshwater habitats, such as rivers and estuaries, is not as great as in the world's seas. All freshwater creatures began life in the sea, and developed from marine creatures millions of years ago. Many belong to the same families that live today in marine environments. The freshwater crustaceans, mollusks, and turtles all have bodies which successfully adapted to freshwater life. Their habits have adapted, too, enabling them to go upstream from the seas and maintain their ground against the constant flow of water and strong currents. Many freshwater creatures lay eggs that can be secured to plants, or give birth to live young - the free-swimming larvae common to many sea creatures would have no chance of survival, and would be washed away downstream toward the sea.

**FRESHWATER LOBSTER**
Crayfish live in freshwater habitats in many parts of the world - in Louisiana, they are a staple of Cajun cooking. They tend to live under stones or in shallow burrows. Most crayfish will lie low until a small fish or some other tempting morsel passes by, and then will snap it up in their powerful claws. Not all crayfish are active the whole year round - some dig deep burrows in which they remain all winter; others swim out to deeper waters and lie on the bottom until the weather warms again.

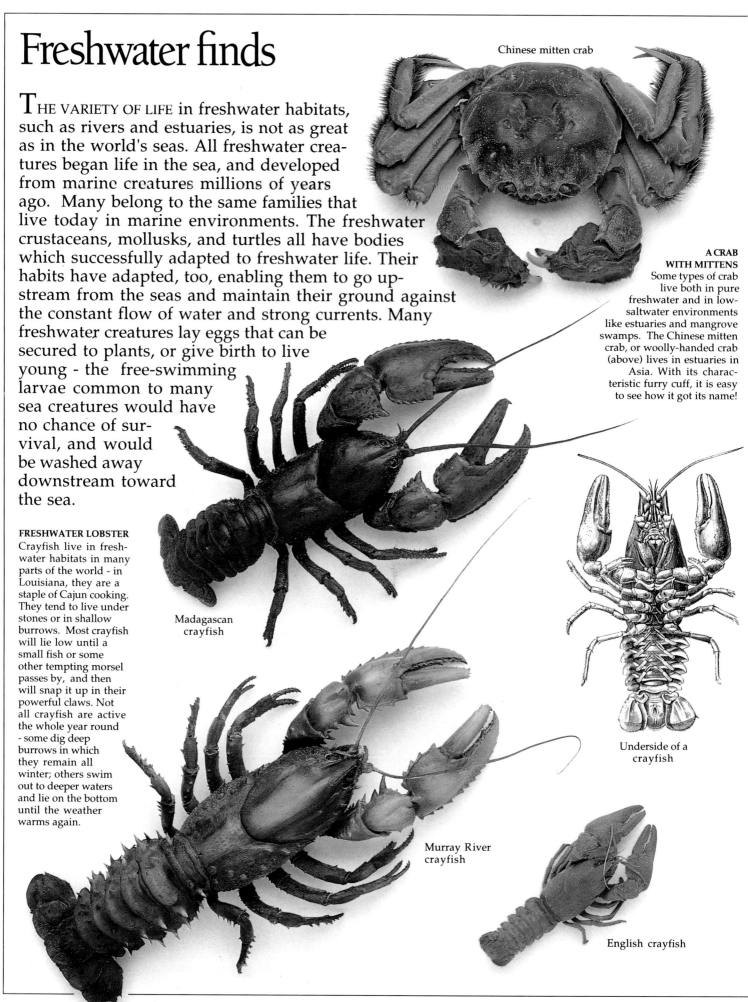

Chinese mitten crab

**A CRAB WITH MITTENS**
Some types of crab live both in pure freshwater and in low-saltwater environments like estuaries and mangrove swamps. The Chinese mitten crab, or woolly-handed crab (above) lives in estuaries in Asia. With its characteristic furry cuff, it is easy to see how it got its name!

Madagascan crayfish

Underside of a crayfish

Murray River crayfish

English crayfish

**A REAL SOFTIE**
Most members of the tortoise
family have hardened carapaces, but
the spiny soft-shelled river turtle
from North America has a rounded,
flexible carapace with no bony plates at
all. Unlike other members of its family,
the soft-shell is able to move fast
both in water and on land.

**TURTLE OR TERRAPIN?**
The only real difference between a turtle
and a terrapin is its habitat. The
European pond turtle is one of over
80 species of mainly freshwater
turtles living today. A
meat-eating turtle, it
hunts both in the water
and on land, feeding
on small fish,
worms, mollusks,
and frogs.

European
pond turtle

**SNAPPING, NOT NAPPING**
The alligator snapping turtle is one of the most
bizarre-looking of all the turtles. It catches
prey by lying totally still on the river bed,
huge mouth agape. Within its mouth is
a fleshy, pink appendage that looks like
a wriggling worm. Any unsuspecting fish
that takes this "bait" finds instant death
between the turtle's powerful, snapping jaws.
The alligator snapping turtle inhabits deep
rivers and lakes of central North America,
where it is often caught for food (right).

South American
ram's-horn snails

Alligator snapping
turtle farm

Giant
Amazonian
river snail

Giant
Venezuelan
river snail

African freshwater
"oyster"

**FRESHWATER MOLLUSKS**
Mollusks living in freshwater environments tend to have
lighter, thinner shells than marine ones and are less
colorful, enabling them to blend in well with their
surroundings. Freshwater gastropods come in all shapes
and sizes, the largest ones being the river snails of the Amazon
(South America) and some areas of Africa (above). Gastropods and
bivalves are the only types of mollusk that live in freshwater.

# Inland inhabitants

Mᴏsᴛ ᴋɪɴᴅs ᴏf sʜᴇʟʟᴇᴅ ᴄʀᴇᴀᴛᴜʀᴇs make their homes in the world's oceans. But there are some that have emerged slowly from the sea over millions of years and evolved to live on land. Among the most successful of these creatures are the mollusks, including many thousands of different types of land snail that live in environments as diverse as deserts and tropical rain forests. Some live high up in the branches of the forest canopy; others can be found several feet underground. A few crustaceans and some reptiles also have adapted successfully to the land; the slow-moving tortoises are the only reptiles that have needed to keep a protective outer shell.

Coconut husk broken by robber crab

*Powerful claws*

*Strengthened carapace*

**CRABS IN THE TREES**
The robber, or "coconut," crab can be found on some Pacific islands. A tree-climbing giant, it can grow up to 18 in (45 cm) long and climbs trees in search of coconuts, which it cracks open with its powerful claws. As a young adult, the crab carries a mollusk shell, like a hermit crab, and when it has outgrown this, it carries half a coconut! Eventually, it relies on its claws and hardened exoskeleton for protection. On some islands, the crab is hunted for food. When caught, however, the robber crab must be held carefully to avoid serious injury, as this Cook Islander (left) is demonstrating .

58

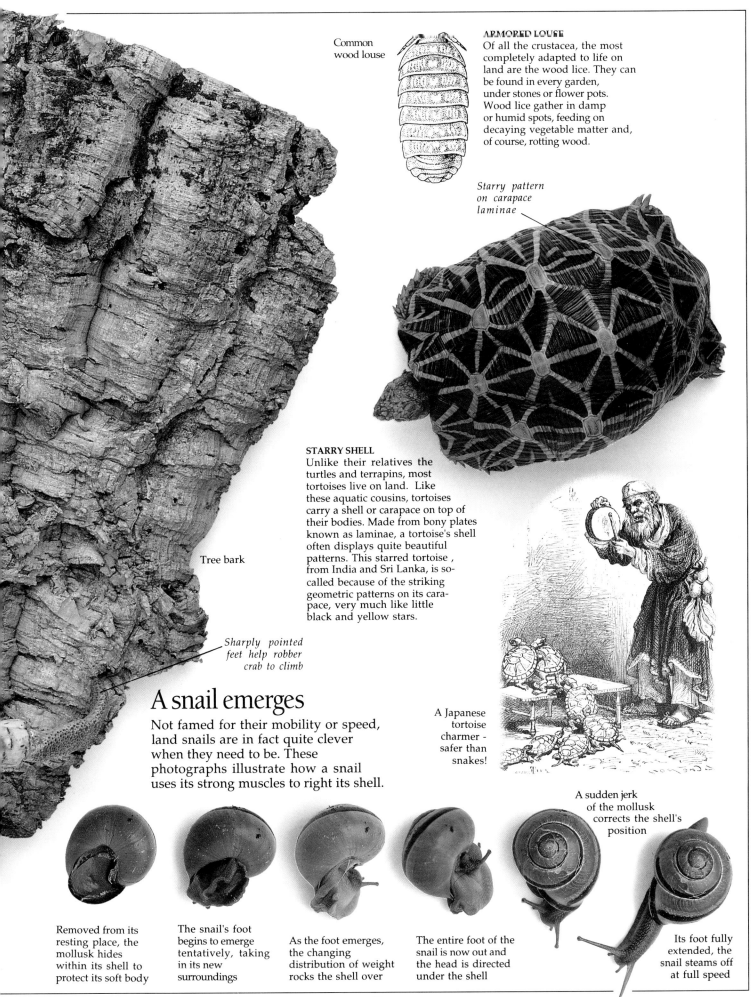

Common
wood louse

**ARMORED LOUSE**
Of all the crustacea, the most
completely adapted to life on
land are the wood lice. They can
be found in every garden,
under stones or flower pots.
Wood lice gather in damp
or humid spots, feeding on
decaying vegetable matter and,
of course, rotting wood.

*Starry pattern
on carapace
laminae*

**STARRY SHELL**
Unlike their relatives the
turtles and terrapins, most
tortoises live on land. Like
these aquatic cousins, tortoises
carry a shell or carapace on top of
their bodies. Made from bony plates
known as laminae, a tortoise's shell
often displays quite beautiful
patterns. This starred tortoise ,
from India and Sri Lanka, is so-
called because of the striking
geometric patterns on its carapace, very much like little
black and yellow stars.

Tree bark

*Sharply pointed
feet help robber
crab to climb*

## A snail emerges

Not famed for their mobility or speed,
land snails are in fact quite clever
when they need to be. These
photographs illustrate how a snail
uses its strong muscles to right its shell.

A Japanese
tortoise
charmer -
safer than
snakes!

A sudden jerk
of the mollusk
corrects the shell's
position

Removed from its
resting place, the
mollusk hides
within its shell to
protect its soft body

The snail's foot
begins to emerge
tentatively, taking
in its new
surroundings

As the foot emerges,
the changing
distribution of weight
rocks the shell over

The entire foot of the
snail is now out and
the head is directed
under the shell

Its foot fully
extended, the
snail steams off
at full speed

# Shells in strange places

IN THE CONSTANT STRUGGLE FOR SURVIVAL, plants and animals have evolved to occupy a great variety of land, freshwater, and marine environments. In the world of shelled creatures, there are many peculiar habitats that are occupied by only one type of shelled animal. Many of these animals have learned that the best way to survive is not to be too fussy - barnacles and some types of worm are concerned only with having a solid base on which to live. Some animals have developed close associations with other creatures and in fact live off them; others will cling to almost any secure surface they can find.

Brachiopod, or lampshell

**LINGERING LAMPSHELL**
Brachiopods, or lampshells, attach themselves to solid surfaces by means of a flexible stalk, and can sometimes be found living on mollusk shells, as here.

Barnacles

**COCKLE COLONY**
Covering this empty cockle shell are hundreds of white shelly tubes made by a type of marine worm. These worms attach themselves to almost any solid surface available, and often live in large colonies. They extend their tentacles from the end of the tubes to catch particles of food that float past.

*Calcareous worm tubes*

*Mollusk*

Worm tube on a top shell

*Mollusk shell*

**IN A SPIN**
As if wanting to imitate its shelled partner, this worm tube has slowly followed the spiral coiling of the mollusk on which it sits.

**MIXED MOLLUSKS**
This thorny oyster, a bivalve mollusk, has two very different types of marine animal attached to its shell. Although the white shelly tubes are all worm-shaped, the largest one actually belongs to a gastropod mollusk.

*Worm tubes*

**SITTING ON THE POT**
Submerged underwater for about 2,000 years, this Roman two-handled jar (right) has probably played host to thousands of different marine creatures. There are three distinct types visible here: barnacles, worm tubes, and mollusks.

Goose barnacles

## SHELLY SHIPWRECKERS

Much as termites will eat through wood on land, teredo shipworms will do equal damage to timber in the sea, and have long been the scourge of wooden-ship builders. Although called a shipworm, it is actually a bivalve mollusk that makes the holes and the shelly tubes they contain. The mollusk's tiny shell is used more as a drilling tool than for protection.

*Holes made by shipworms*

Shelly tubes of shipworm removed from wood

Shipworms often had a devastating effect on early sailing ships

Helmet shell

## HIDEAWAY HERMIT

The hermit crab (right), often seen in shallow water pools, is not the natural inhabitant of the shell in which it lives. This crab does not possess a hard shell of its own, so it "borrows" an empty mollusk shell and, as it grows, discards its home in favor of a more spacious one.

Common hermit crab

Roman jar

Scallop shell embedded in sponge

## COMFORTABLE ACCOMMODATION

Some shells can even be found embedded in soft sections of natural sponge. This is often because the sponge grew over a dead shell, but sometimes a mollusk will deliberately select this soft site as its home, as in the case of the scallop shell seen here.

## IS IT A BIRD....?

Goose barnacles are crustaceans that can live, attached by a stalk, to almost any object floating in the sea - including the hulls of boats and ships. Goose barnacles are so-called because of the similarity between their shells and fleshy stalks and the white head and black neck of a certain type of goose. It used to be thought that the barnacles "grew up" and turned into birds.

Goose barnacles

Barnacle goose

# Collecting shells

SHELL COLLECTING IS A POPULAR and satisfying hobby, and a walk along the beach may be enough to start a collection. It is sometimes tempting to collect living creatures, as their shells are often in better condition than those that have been tossed about by waves or weathered by the elements. But check the local laws first - it is illegal in some places to collect live specimens. Treat everything you touch with care, and, if you are overturning rocks or coral slabs to look underneath, make sure you return them to their original position.

**ON THE BEACH**
Rock pools are often teeming with life, and shells that would normally only be found in deeper waters are sometimes stranded there. It pays to look closely, as many creatures seek the darkness and moisture found in rock crevices or underneath stones.

**COLLECTING UNDERWATER**
Collecting underwater reveals many shells in their natural habitats. You can use a snorkel in shallow waters, and, with proper training, scuba diving will open up a new world.

Plastic collecting bags

Mask and snorkel

**TOOLS OF THE TRADE**
A keen pair of eyes is the first thing needed by the collector, as living shells seldom display the bright colors seen in collections. A knife is useful for prying shells off rocks (ask an adult to help you), and some kind of collecting bag is essential. Sieves with a range of mesh sizes enable you quickly to separate shells of different sizes.

Strong penknife

Shells, rocks, and weeds separated from sand

Sieve for sorting small shells from sand

Tweezers

Sharp knife
or scalpel

Uncleaned
specimen

Magnifying
glasses

Identification
reference book

Cotton
swabs

Cleaned
specimen

*More elongated
shape and lack
of dark markings
between ribs*

*Clearly defined
markings
between ribs*

*Heavier shell
with more
angular shape*

Achromatic Lens
10X

**CLEANING SPECIMENS**
It is usually best to clean the shells
fairly soon after they have been
collected. The shells can
be soaked for a few hours in
a 50/50 solution of household
bleach and water, then scrubbed.

**IDENTITY PARADE**
Examining shells with a magnifying glass or microscope
will reveal details that will help to identify them
correctly; for example, the three shells shown above are
very similar but are in fact all separate species. Most
shells have a name by which experts can identify them,
and you will need to refer to specialist guides
to name your collection.

Dental tool
for cleaning

Old tooth-
brush for
scrubbing

Labels

**STORING
AND CATALOGING**
When you are out
collecting, always take a
notebook and record as much
information as possible about
each animal. Later, you can write
up these details in a catalog and
label your specimens with the page
number. Most shells fade when
exposed to light, so store them
in the dark. Shallow
drawers are useful for
most types of shell, and you
can use small boxes or film
canisters to divide types
within drawers.

Transparent plastic
boxes and film canister
for storage

*Plastic boxes with
identification
labels
underneath*

*Locality
data*

# Index

# Acknowledgements

**Dorling Kindersley would like to thank:**
David Attard (Malta), Andrew Clarke (British Antarctic Survey); Derek Coombes; Geoff Cox, Koën Fraussen (Belgium); Dr. Ray Ingle, Dr. Roger Lincoln, Colin McCarthy, Chris Owen, and Andrew Stimson of the British Museum (Natural History); Samuel Jones (Pearls) Ltd.; Sue Mennell; Alistair Moncur; José Maria Hernandez Otero (Spain); Tom and Celia Pain; Respectable Reptiles; Alan Seccombe; Dr. Francisco Garcia Talavera, Museum of Santa Cruz (Natural History); Ken Wye (Eaton's Shell Shop); John Youles.

Lynn Bresler for the index
Mike Pilley and Fred Ford of Radius Graphics
Karl Shone for special photography on pages 6-7 and 40-41
Jane Burton for special photography on page 59

**Picture credits**
(t=top, b=bottom, m=middle, l=left, r=right)
Doug Allan: 26
The Ancient Art & Architecture Collection: 44br
Heather Angel: 20, 25, 40tl & mr, 46tr, 54tl
Ardea London: 29tr, 35mr
Axel Poignant Archive: 39MR
BBC Hulton Picture Library: 37T&BL
The Bridgeman Art Library/Uffizi Gallery, Florence: 16
The Bridgeman Art Library/Alan Jacobs Gallery, London: 22tr
Bruce Coleman Ltd.: 7tr
Mary Evans Picture Library: 8, 11, 12, 15, 19br, 22br, 26tl, 28tl, 30tr, 34tl & mr, 36br, 50tl, 57 tl & mr, 59mr
The Kobal Collection/20th-Century

Fox: 14
National Museum of Wales: 38bl
Planet Earth Pictures/Seaphot: 19ml, 24br, 27, 42, 52tl, 53tm& bm, 58bl
Rothschild Estate: 30BR
Robert Harding Picture Library: 55bl 54, 56, 58

**Illustrators:** Will Giles, Sandra Pond: 21b; 35t; 43b;